A 12-SESSION GROUP TREATMENT PROGRAM

Healing

FOR ADULT

Survivors

OF CHILDHOOD

Sexual
Abuse

Healing

FOR ADULT

Survivors

OF CHILDHOOD

Sexual

Abuse

Bonnie Collins, Ed.M., C.S.W.-R
Kathryn Marsh, C.S.W.-R

WHOLE PERSON ASSOCIATES
Duluth, Minnesota

REPRODUCTION POLICY

Unless otherwise noted, your purchase of this volume entitles you to reproduce a modest quantity of the worksheets that appear in this book for your education and training activities. For this limited worksheet reproduction, no special additional permission is needed. However the following statement, in total, must appear on all copies that you reproduce.

Specific prior written permission is required from the publisher for any reproduction of a complete or adapted exercise with trainer instructions, or large-scale reproduction of worksheets, or for inclusion of material in another publication. Licensing or royalty arrangement requests for this usage must be submitted in writing and approved prior to any such use.

For further information, please write for our Permissions Guidelines and Standard Permissions Form. Permission requests must be submitted at least thirty days in advance of your scheduled printing or reproduction.

Library of Congress Cataloging in Publication Data

Collins, Bonnie J.
Healing for adult survivors of childhood sexual abuse : a 12-session group treatment program / Bonnie J. Collins and Kathryn Marsh.
144 p. 23 cm.

ISBN 1-57025-165-7
1. Adult child sexual abuse victims—Rehabilitation. 2. Adult child sexual abuse victims—Mental health. 3. Adult child sexual abuse victims—Family relationships. I. Marsh, Kathryn. II. Title.
RC569.5.A28 C63 1998
616.85'8369—ddc21   98-8937
                                                                        CIP

Printed in the United States of America

10 9 8 7 6 5 4 3 2 1

Whole Person Associates, Inc.
210 West Michigan
Duluth MN 55802-1908 218-727-0500
Web site: http://www.wholeperson.com
E-mail: books@wholeperson.com

We dedicate this work to Jennifer,
and to all Survivors,
whose courage we honor . . .

Table of Contents

Often the process of beginning to share events of past abuse can open the floodgates of feelings for survivors. This is such a critical aspect of the entire healing process that facilitators need to offer the time required for participants to talk about the impact on their own individual healing process of breaking their secret. Therefore, two sessions dealing with this topic are often required. If necessary, repeat this session until everyone has told her story.

Participants are beginning to realize that "the only way out is through." In this session, they will further examine the theme of shame and how it binds survivors to the abuse and keeps them from healing.

The next two sessions focus on helping survivors to experience the part of themselves that they typically repressed in order to survive their childhood. These sessions are critical to the healing process. They allow survivors to recover the part of themselves that, because of the abuse they suffered, never had an opportunity to grow and flourish. We refer to this part as the "child within." This is the part of all human beings that allows them to laugh, to cry, to feel joy, anxiety, love, and peace. For healing to occur, survivors need to be given explicit permission to feel their feelings and express them. Expressing within the group what was difficult to express as an abused child will allow survivors to welcome feelings into their daily lives.

©1998 Whole Person Associates 210 W Michigan Duluth MN 55802   (800) 247-6789

This session continues with the theme of the child within. Most survivors have learned to repress their feelings in order to protect themselves from hurt and pain. It is the child within who holds those feelings, waiting for permission to express them.

In this session, survivors are helped to see that the anger that they have internalized (often felt as rage) is justified. Facilitators support their need to release this anger, suggest safe ways to do this, and provide boundaries so survivors can maintain a sense of control during this process.

In the previous sessions, participants experienced the process of finding the child within, communicating with her, and making her feel as safe as possible. They now have an opportunity to express anger toward their abusers in a healthy way. Participants are now ready to explore the theme of confronting their abuser.

Exploring confrontation in a group can be a powerful healing experience. Therefore, even though participants may have already confronted their abuser on their own or have decided they will never confront their abuser, encourage them to participate fully in this session.

Through role play, each participant has the opportunity to rehearse what she would say and do if she were to confront her abuser in real life. Supported by the group, survivors are empowered to make healthy choices concerning confrontation of their abuser.

The theme of grief and loss is important in the healing process. We have found that many abuse survivors resist feeling sadness and loss. When these feelings come to the surface and are dealt with, survivors can then let go of their experience of abuse and grow, develop, and thrive.

The last session of this group for survivors is designed to provide an opportunity to "do endings" in a different way than perhaps they have had the opportunity to do before.

To give participants time to work on their individual healing goals and to prepare to say good-bye to the group, the session is deliberately delayed for two weeks after the eleventh session.

Significant others may include partners, siblings, close friends, or relatives who have an interest in learning more about the effects of past abuse on the survivor and who would like to better understand the process of healing, particularly as it unfolds in the group process. Survivors use a letter to extend the invitation to whomever they wish to participate in this session. The survivors themselves do not attend the session. Facilitators must, therefore, respect their privacy and speak only in generic terms as they discuss particular themes in the healing process. Specific information about each survivor's story must be kept confidential.

©1998 Whole Person Associates 210 W Michigan Duluth MN 55802   (800) 247-6789

About the Authors

Bonnie Collins is a marriage and family counselor in practice in Hamburg, New York. She provides family systems therapy to individuals, couples, and families, specializing in short-term therapy for adult survivors of childhood sexual abuse. In addition to her 28 years of experience as a therapist, she is also a consultant to scores of private and corporate clients and adjunct faculty at the School of Social Work SUNY at Buffalo.

Kathryn Marsh is a clinical supervisor with Catholic Charities in Buffalo, New York and an AAMFT approved supervisor. She supervises the work of therapists who provide services to children and parents with a history of abuse and neglect. Since 1989, she has cofacilitated 12-week therapy groups for adult survivors of incest.

©1998 Whole Person Associates 210 W Michigan Duluth MN 55802   (800) 247-6789

Acknowledgments

We would like to acknowledge the following people for assisting us in the creation of this book:

The other clinicians who have facilitated groups with us—Linda Abrams, CSW, CSAC, and Sharon Herlehy, RN, RH, CSW. We would like to thank Linda for her creative spirit in helping us design some of our most meaningful experiential exercises for the group, and Sharon for her wonderful clinical wisdom.

And most of all, Kathy Pipitone, BA, CD, for her hard work, patience, and loving support in getting it all down on paper!

And of course, our editor, Susan Gustafson, who felt like a friend throughout this process.

©1998 Whole Person Associates 210 W Michigan Duluth MN 55802   (800) 247-6789

Introduction

Alarmingly, significant numbers of both men and women report having been sexually abused as children. The term "child sexual abuse" refers to sexual contact between a child and an individual in a position of power and authority. Published estimates of the prevalence of childhood sexual abuse range from 15 to 33 percent for females (e.g., Freeman-Longo & Blanchard, 1997; Finkelhor, Hoteling, Lewis & Smith, 1990; Briere & Runtz, 1989, and 13 to 16 percent for males (e.g., Finkelhor et al., Fromouth & Burkart, 1989.) Studies have shown that the majority of child victims are female and that one in five children may be sexually abused prior to age eighteen. (Freeman-Longo & Blanchard, 1997)

Incest is the sexual abuse of a child by a parental figure, e.g., a father, mother, stepparent, or sibling. Incest is particularly devastating exploitation of children because it is a betrayal of a primary trust. The long-term psychological effects have been well documented; they include depression, anxiety, interpersonal problems, dissociative experiences, suicide, and sexual dysfunctions.

Group treatment for sexual abuse survivors provides an important comple-ment to individual therapy (Reicher, 1994; Mennen & Meadow, 1993) Problems such as social isolation, difficulties with intimacy, and mistrust of others are particularly well addressed in a group setting. Understanding that they are not alone, gaining acceptance from others, experiencing the oppor-tunity to engage in meaningful social relationships, and practicing intimacy are but a few of the distinct advantages of membership in a treatment group.

We have written this manual as a guide for professional therapists who are interested in providing a short-term, time-limited (12 weeks) structured, therapeutic group experience for survivors of childhood sexual abuse. While most of the survivors we treated were incest victims, this model and the themes dealt with are relevant to all adult survivors of sexual abuse.

The model was developed over a period of eight years, during which time we treated more than two hundred survivors in a group setting. Our clients

©1998 Whole Person Associates 210 W Michigan Duluth MN 55802
(800) 247-6789

taught us what was useful to them. In response, we modified and refined the processes. Many of the exercises were developed as a result of specific issues and needs raised directly by the survivors themselves. We are pleased now to be able to offer what we have learned to other professionals who choose to work with this very special population.

Working with survivors of childhood sexual abuse has been one of the most challenging yet rewarding experiences we have had as therapists. The female survivors of childhood sexual abuse who have participated in our groups are some of the strongest women we have ever met. We honor their courage and their ability to move on and live full and rich lives. We thank them for the opportunity to be a part of their healing journeys and for all the ways they have enriched our spirits. Our goal for these courageous survivors is that they recover their lives rather than spend their lives recovering!

Suggestions for using this manual

We would like to stress a few important points about working with survivors of childhood sexual abuse.

We feel strongly that this kind of group needs to be led by two facilitators. However, we understand, practically speaking that this is not always possible. You may find yourself leading such a group alone. In that case, we need to stress how important it is to get good clinical supervision.

Facilitators are most successful when they are authentic, when they offer hope and optimism, and when they encourage empowerment of the survivor.

It is necessary to maintain a balance between structure and flexibility. Showing compassion towards participants and always giving them choices helps them appreciate this structure and flexibility.

Chapters in this manual are built around specific themes that we have found to be critical in the group treatment of adult survivors. Although we present these themes in a linear way, each theme being dealt with in a separate session, effective group facilitators will be responsive to the group's concerns. In this way, survivors will experience an integrated healing process that respects both the individual's and group's needs.

©1998 Whole Person Associates 210 W Michigan Duluth MN 55802   (800) 247-6789

It is important to be aware that this healing journey is a *developmental process* and the sessions are designed to be used in the order in which they are presented. We advise that a clinician not try any of the exercises out of order.

Each session follows a standard format:

- Grounding and centering

- Processing homework

- Information and experiential exercise developing the theme of the session

- Homework assignment preparation for the next session

- Closing ritual

Throughout the book, you will find convenient outlines for mini-lectures along with lists of discussion questions. You will want to review this material carefully so you can modify and expand on it to fit your own experience.

Creating a welcoming environment

Survivors who are starting a group healing experience usually approach the first group session with fear, anxiety, and reluctance. For many survivors entering a group triggers an emotional memory of their first experience in a group, that of their family. It is important, therefore, for group facilitators to establish an environment that is as welcoming and safe as possible.

The following ideas will help you make your environment welcoming.

- Have coffee, tea, and water available as participants arrive.

- Play soft, soothing background music.

- Use soft lights to create a warm atmosphere.

- Welcome the participants as a hostess welcomes guests into her home.

©1998 Whole Person Associates 210 W Michigan Duluth MN 55802 (800) 247-6789

1 Setting the Stage

In a welcoming environment, participants are encouraged to consider what they need to feel comfortable and safe. They review the group's goals and begin setting personal goals.

Goals

To introduce participants to each other.

To help them feel secure in the group.

To introduce them to the group's goals.

Materials

Pocket folders; paper and pens; **Take Care of Yourself** handout; **Group Guidelines** handout; **Group Goals** handout; **Magic Wand** worksheet.

> ☞*Provide a folder for each participant that includes the handouts for this session, paper, and pen. This will give them an opportunity to have something to look at as they wait for others to arrive and will help them lower their natural anxieties about being in a group for survivors.*

Welcome

As participants enter the room, invite them to choose the seat they would feel most comfortable in.

> ☞*If possible, provide soft, sink-in chairs as well as hard-backed chairs. To help survivors feel comfortable and secure, arrange the seating so some chairs are close to doors and walls.*

When all participants have settled themselves, introduce yourself and welcome them as a group, making the following comments:

- Congratulations on having the courage to be part of this group.

- Your decision to join the group was probably difficult to make, but it's a very important step in your healing process.

- Sitting here in an unfamiliar room with people you don't know, you may feel a bit like a "stranger in a strange land."

Encourage participants to select an object that will help them feel more secure and to say a few words about it.

- To help yourself feel more comfortable, look around the room and select an object that has a pleasant association for you; or, if you prefer, reach into your pocket or purse and find an item that you can hold for security as we move forward.

Introductions

As a nonthreatening warm-up activity that allows participants to share as little or as much as they want about themselves, ask them to talk for a minute about their first name.

- To help us become acquainted with each other, I'd like each of you to share your first name with the group along with a memory or association that is connected with your name.

- You might want to tell us how you were given your name, who you were named after, or what you like or don't like about your name.

> ☞ *To help participants break the ice and become more person-ally involved with the group, begin by giving your name and an association connected with it.*

Establishing safety

Establishing safety in a survivors' group is critical to the successful achievement of all goals. The following exercise is important because it empowers participants to create a safe environment for themselves.

During the discussion, group cohesiveness and supportive bonding begin to be established.

Provide the following introduction and instructions:

- For you to get the most benefit from participation in this group, it's important that you feel comfortable and safe.

- Determining what makes you feel safe here will help you consider what will make you feel safe outside our group.

- Take a piece of paper and a pen from your folder and spend the next 5 minutes thinking, then writing, what you need from the group in order for you to feel safe.

☞Play background music softly as participants work.

After 5 minutes, or when all appear to be finished writing, lead a discussion, asking each survivor to share as much or as little of what they have written as they feel comfortable sharing. Call attention to similarities and differences in their responses.

Ask participants to take the **Group Guidelines** handout from their folder. After discussing whether any of the guidelines need to be modified, ask members to commit to them.

Ask participants to discuss the methods they now use to feel safe outside the group and encourage them to expand their repertoire with some of the ideas that others have shared.

Draw the attention of participants to the **Take Care of Yourself** hand-out and suggest that they review it regularly to remind themselves that they are entitled to take care of themselves.

Goal setting and homework

Establishing individual and group goals is an important part of keeping a group on task and focused. It helps participants feel safe since they will have a better understanding of what to expect.

Tell participants to take the **Group Goals** handout from their folders and lead a brief discussion about them. These goals outline the facilitator's agenda and may well trigger ideas for individual participant goals.

Present the following homework assignment.

■ It was important for our group to review the goals for our work together; it's equally important that you identify your individual goals.

■ What do you want to be different when this group completes its work together? Take time this week to think about your personal goals for our group experience and list them on the **Magic Wand** worksheet, which you will find in your folder.

■ Then indicate how you will know that you have reached a goal? Be as specific as possible. For example, if you feel depressed, you may sleep very late on weekends because nothing interests you. Getting up earlier would be a sign that your depression is lifting.

■ During the next session, we will spend time sharing individual goals with the whole group.

Closing ritual of sharing and support

Closing rituals provide a consistent structure for bringing the group to a close. These can be very important for participants who need to establish a safe boundary between the often painful work of the group and returning to the realities of their everyday life. Select your own ritual, or use our favorite, which follows:

■ Please stand and gather in a circle. If you would like, take the hand of the person next to you.

> ☞*Often it takes a few sessions before some survivors feel safe enough to hold hands.*

■ For the next few minutes, let's share with each other some of the special things that happened within our group.

> ☞ *You can also use this time to emphasize any themes or ideas that may promote healing for the group members e.g. , "I was struck today by how courageous each of you were in sharing some painful memories with each other," or "I am very impressed with how each of you are able to challenge each other to really reach your goals."*

When everyone who wants to has had an opportunity to speak, raise your hands and say "Ah-women!" as a concluding affirmation.

Be aware of any signs of stress as the group ends. Sometimes it may be necessary to process whatever may be bothering a survivor before she starts for home in order to assure her safety as well as to prevent unnecessary anxiety between sessions.

Take Care of Yourself

Ask for what you want . . . use "I" messages.

Say NO when you choose.

Listen to music.

Open your eyes to the beauty of nature.

Spend time with people who help you FEEL GOOD about yourself.

Appreciate your body . . . it is good.

Eat healthy foods . . . exercise.

Make time to laugh and play!

Nurture your friends . . . and pets.

Keep a journal.

Kick a pillow.

Hug yourself . . . and others.

Be patient with yourself.

Open yourself up to a higher power.

Say "thank you" to compliments.

Love yourself . . . YOU DESERVE IT!!!

©1998 Whole Person Associates 210 W Michigan Duluth MN 55802   (800) 247-6789

Group Guidelines

1. Group members are expected to attend each meeting. This is important for the successful achievement of trust, positive bonding, and safety of group participants. If it becomes necessary to miss a session, members are expected to telephone one of the group facilitators and explain why they cannot attend. Any group member who misses more than two meetings *may* be asked to leave the group but will be welcome to reapply for a later group.

2. Members are required to continue with their individual counseling throughout the course of the group. Although members are encouraged to continue with any support group they attend, such as Alcoholics Anonymous, joining an additional therapy group during this 12-week period is discouraged.

3. Counseling services will be coordinated between the individual counselor and the group leaders.

4. All information shared in the group **will be kept confidential by the group facilitators and members**, except in situations in which a group member has given written permission to share information or in life threatening or child abuse situations.

5. Interaction among participants outside of group is discouraged. If any significant interaction does occur, it is the responsibility of those involved to see that the content of the interaction is brought back to the group and discussed.

Group Goals

In this healing group, we will:

1. Find a safe environment in which to share our stories.

2. Learn to identify and express emotions connected with our trauma.

3. Eliminate feelings of being responsible for our abuse.

4. Acknowledge the abuse and grieve our childhood losses.

5. Reevaluate our abuse experiences and their meanings by seeing them in a new context.

6. Feel empowered as survivors.

7. Increase our sense of worth and competence.

8. Reduce any self-destructive behavior patterns.

9. Develop new, adaptive behavior patterns.

10. Reduce our isolation and increase our affiliation with others.

Magic Wand

If I could wave a magic wand, how will I be different as a result of this group experience?

1. I will _____

_____

_____

I will know I have achieved this when _____

_____

_____

2. I will _____

_____

_____

I will know I have achieved this when _____

_____

_____

3. I will _____

_____

_____

I will know I have achieved this when _____

_____

_____

2   Determining Goals

Survivors of sexual abuse often grow up in home environments that lack consistency and structure. Feelings of anxiety, helplessness, and hopelessness can result from a chaotic, unpredictable environment. In this session, facilitators empower participants by structuring a goal setting process that allows for the identification and exchange of each participant's individual goals for healing.

Goals

To develop, share, and commit to achievable goals.

To continue group bonding.

To prepare to share a memory of abuse in the next session.

Materials

Writing Your Story handout; **Journaling Techniques** handout.

Check-in

At the beginning of each session, a brief check-in will encourage group bonding.

Greet participants as they enter the room, encouraging them to select a seat they will be comfortable in. When all participants have arrived, take a quick "group pulse," using some of the following questions to stimulate discussion:

> ☞ *Keep the check-in brief and focused on the topic of this group experience. Gently redirect discussion of marital problems or other issues that don't relate to the healing process.*

■ How are you feeling about your experience in this group so far?

- Can you identify some of the specific feelings you had during or after the last session?

- Are you more or less comfortable than you had anticipated?

- Do you have any specific concerns you'd like to talk about? If you're feeling anxious, chances are others in the group share your fears and would find a discussion helpful.

Conclude the check-in process with supportive, empowering comments about participants' courage as they continue their individual healing process.

Goals for healing

In preparation for this session, participants were asked to identify three wishes or goals for healing along with signs that would indicate the goals had been achieved. Identifying and stating these positive behavioral changes in the group setting creates a strong sense of possibility for all of the participants. Having these positive, achievable goals written on newsprint also anchors for participants the importance of their full participation in the work of the group.

Present the following introduction to the activity:

- During our last session together, you were asked to identify three wishes or goals for your healing process. You were also asked to consider how you would know that your goals had been achieved.

- Today, you will each have a chance to share your three goals with other members of our group. After you state each goal, we'll work with you to be sure that your goal can be reached. We'll be asking one another, "How will you know when you attain this goal?"

As each participant states her goals, write them on a sheet of newsprint (one for each person), then tape the lists on the wall where they can be referred to from week to week.

Help participants be clear and specific as goals are identified. When all participants goals are posted, lead a discussion which compares similarities and differences.

Homework

The next stage of healing requires that participants begin telling the story of their abuse. As you introduce the homework assignment, look for and respond to signs of anxiety and continue to promote a safe and healing environment.

Be aware of the range of differences among participants. Some may have told their story of abuse many times. Others have told it only to their individual therapist. It is important to normalize these differences.

Distribute the **Writing Your Story** and **Journaling Techniques** handouts as a guide for completing the homework. Then introduce the assignment with the following thoughts:

- You may have kept the secret of your abuse for many years, believing it was too painful or shameful to share.

- For you to continue in your healing process, it's essential that you begin telling your story in a safe and supportive environment.

- In preparation for this, begin to put your story on paper, using the process outlined on the **Writing Your Story** handout.

    Get comfortable in an environment where you feel safe.

    Don't worry about spelling, grammar, etc.

    Use the writing as a way to **release** the story from you.

    Include sensory details: what you remember seeing, hearing, tasting, touching, and smelling.

    When you come to memories that seem too painful or shameful to reveal, write them anyway.

    Be honest with yourself.

    Don't judge or censor yourself.

- If you have difficulty getting started with the writing process, try some of the suggestions on the **Journaling Techniques** handout. Or, if you prefer, draw or paint your memories.

- When you have completed writing or drawing at least one detailed memory, celebrate your success.

- Prior to our next meeting, read through what you have written and determine what specific memory you feel ready to share with the group.

- Remember that you have choices—you can decide which memories you feel comfortable talking about and which are still too painful to share.

Closing ritual

As participants join in the closing ritual, encourage a discussion of ways they can feel safe as they complete their challenging homework assignment. Remind them that they have the power to make choices about what they do and don't want to share.

- Please stand and gather in a circle. If you would like to, take the hand of the person next to you.

- For the next few minutes, let's share with each other some of the special things that happened within our group.

- If you have any concerns about the writing you'll be doing this week or the sharing you've been asked to do next week, let's talk about them now.

When everyone who wants to has had an opportunity to speak, raise your hands and say "Ah-women!" as a concluding affirmation.

Writing Your Story

Telling your story, breaking the secret of your abuse, is an act that will liberate you. This step is **critical** to your healing process. It requires **courage from you** and **support from the group**.

Putting your story on paper can help you get ready to share it with others. Here are some suggestions as you begin:

■ Get comfortable in an environment where you feel safe.

■ Don't worry about spelling, grammar etc.

■ Use the writing as a way to **release** the story from you.

■ Include sensory details: what you remember seeing, hearing, tasting, touching, and smelling.

■ When you come to memories that seem too painful or shameful to reveal, write them anyway.

■ Be honest with yourself.

■ Don't judge or censor yourself.

■ If you have difficulty getting started with the writing process, try some of the suggestions on the **Journaling Techniques** handout. Or, if you prefer, draw or paint your memories.

When you have completed writing at least one detailed memory, celebrate your success.

Come to the next session prepared to share any part of this story that you choose. **Remember, you have choices and you are in charge of your healing process.** The group facilitators are there to help and support you.

Journaling Techniques

Journaling can help you release anger and explore joys. It is also a way of helping you, a survivor of abuse, identify emotions that as a child, you were told not to feel or were punished for expressing.

In preparation for journaling, treat yourself to a smooth-flowing pen and a journal that is special to you—it could even be homemade. Also create a special time and place for writing that encourages an atmosphere of healing.

The techniques listed below may help you get started:

Lifeline

> Draw a line to represent your life from birth up to the present. Identify positive life events and experiences and record them on top of the line. Record negative experiences under the line. You may need to create more positive experiences in your current life to help balance the negatives of the past.

Safe place imagery

> Describe in writing a special safe place (real or imagined) where you can go to in your "mind's eye" especially when life is stressful. Anchor this written description with a symbolic object like a sea shell, stone, or twig that you can carry in your purse or pocket as a source of reassurance and security.

Dialogue

> Try a conversational style of writing by dialoguing with aspects of yourself, for example your dream figures, your inner child, parts of your body, aspects of your personality, or your wisdom within.

Topic writing

The following topics may be useful to write about as part of your healing process:

My Healing Journey (thus far)

Ways I Take Care of Myself

Special People in My Life

Simple Joys I'm Blessed With

My Successes in Life

Affirmations to Chant to Myself

Problem solving

Use your journal to brainstorm ways to find solutions to your problem. Experts in creative problem solving suggest that defining the problem is the most important step in finding solutions. Also, write down what you've already tried and create a list of new ways to approach the problem. All this writing anchors slippery ideas so they won't get away from you!

3   Breaking the Secret of Abuse

A critical step in healing from childhood sexual abuse is telling the story of what happened and experiencing the repressed feelings from the childhood abuse. Most survivors attending a group have told only their therapist and few, if any, significant others. They have harbored intense feelings of fear, anger, and shame for years. These repressed feelings have isolated them from others and set them apart from the rest of the world. Breaking this secret in a healing group environment allows a survivor to release these feelings and identify with others who have also experienced abuse as children. It often begins the process of sharing with significant others outside the group.

Goals

To release feelings of fear, anger, and shame as the story is told.

To feel empowered, supported, and validated by the group.

Materials

Paper and pencils; crayons or markers.

Grounding and centering

When participants have all made themselves comfortable, present the following activity, pacing your instructions very slowly:

■ We'll begin today by taking a few moments to ground and center ourselves, leaving behind our daily activities and focusing on why we are here together.

■ Place your feet flat on the floor.

■ Rest your hands in your lap.

■ Take a deep breath.

■ Reflect for a moment on why we are here. (pause)

Check-in

Give participants an opportunity to briefly check in. If necessary, remind them that this is a time to discuss feelings and concerns related to the group's work.

Guided imagery

> ☞*Some authors of literature on working with survivors of childhood sexual abuse have raised the concern that visualization exercises with survivors will encourage dissociation and flashbacks. This has not been our experience. If facilitators take the time to prepare the setting and explain the process, then guide the images in a firm voice, using positive language, survivors often express great satisfaction with the experience of visualizing. As long as participants feel they have a choice about this experience, it can be very empowering. (Suggesting that they need not participate gives them permission to join in!) For further information about guided imagery, see the Resources section.*

Physical relaxation

It is usually best to precede any imagery experience with a physical relaxation exercise. Because this may be the participants' first experience with imagery, begin by introducing the concept.

■ Your imagination is very powerful. When you let your imagination run wild, it can frighten you, but by using guided imagery, you can harness the enormous power of your mind, unleash your creativity, change your attitudes, and activate your natural healing powers.

■ As with all activities in this group, you can decide whether or not you want to participate.

■ We'll begin by leading you through a physical relaxation process, then we'll continue with a visualization that will remind you of the many caring people who want to help and support you as you heal.

> ☞*Read the script slowly, pausing briefly between phrases and for a longer time between sentences and paragraphs. When you give an instruction, be sure to give participants plenty of time to complete the action before you move on.*

Relaxation script

Give yourself permission to relax by sitting with your back supported and allow yourself to ground by putting both feet flat on the floor . . . As a way to turn inward, you may want to put your hands in your lap and let your chin rest on your chest . . .

When you feel your eyelids growing heavy, allow your eyes to close . . . a nice way to close out the outside world and feel even more grounded . . . focus inward and relax . . .

Give yourself permission to observe any sounds around you and know you can let them be . . .

Scan your body for tension . . . help it to be comfortable and relaxed . . .

Tune in now to your breathing . . . Notice your own rhythm and how its regularity can soothe you . . . Every once in a while you may wish to take a deep cleansing breath . . . inhaling through your nose and exhaling slowly through your mouth . . . Notice the moment of inner peace at the top of the in-breath before you exhale . . .

This time . . . as you exhale . . . blow out as though you're making a candle flame flicker with your breath . . . long, slow exhale without blowing out the flame . . . again . . . and again.

Imagery script

And now, allow yourself to visualize the images I will describe to you . . . In your mind's eye (your creative imagination) begin to see a mirror . . . a big mirror . . . with a beautiful border of your choosing . . . As you see this mirror more and more clearly, notice your face in it . . . the face you see as you go through your healing . . . your face now, as you are experiencing personal growth . . .

Your face may show some anxiety, but mostly you see in your eyes the hope and courage of a survivor . . .

You may wish to touch the mirror or your own face in a soothing comforting way . . .

Continue to observe your courageous, hopeful face until you also see behind your face in the mirror other supportive faces of significant people in your life . . . Notice as those faces become clearer that they are the faces of people who really care about you and who are traveling your healing journey with you . . .

Identify each one and look clearly to see them all . . . living . . . dead . . . male . . . female . . . young . . . old . . . relatives . . . friends . . . professionals . . . and fellow survivors. Look carefully and gather all those faces behind your face in the mirror . . .

Feel their support . . . in their smiles . . . in their looks of concern . . . in their messages to you. Enjoy their support and feel grateful for their presence in your life . . .

Now, put your left hand on your right wrist as a way to anchor this image . . . This movement will preserve forever this mirror full of significant others. Call on it whenever you feel the need. Just put your left hand on your right wrist wherever you are, whatever you are doing . . . it will bring this image to your creative mind and help you through any of life's crises . . .

Now let go of your wrist and watch the image fade . . . Put your hand back on your wrist and it will come back . . . Notice the good feeling and feel the smile on your face . . . Remember, preserve this anchor forever . . .

Begin to be aware of where you are . . . slowly . . . feel the chair against your back, your feet on the floor . . . you may wish to wiggle your fingers and toes, stretch your neck, hug yourself . . . all before you open your eyes . . . and look around the room.

Anchoring the experience

Drawing or writing about this experience immediately after it takes place and before group discussion can help to further anchor the impact of it. It is most effective not to immediately talk about imagery until group members can anchor it in writing or pictures.

Distribute paper, pencils, markers, and crayons and give the following instructions:

- To help you anchor this experience and make it even easier to recall, spend a few minutes writing or drawing your memory of the visualization or your response to it. (3-5 minutes)

- After looking at what you wrote or drew, please share with the group your experience of this visualization.

Breaking the secret

When the above exercise has concluded, move to the process of breaking the secret. This can be a very difficult experience for both the survivor telling her story and for those listening. Prepare participants with the following instructions:

> ☞ *You as a facilitator may need to help the survivor focus on the specific incident of abuse and the feelings associated with it. Some survivors tell their whole history and thus attempt to avoid the intense feelings that need expressing.*

- This week, you were asked to write out the story of your abuse and to prepare yourself to tell some part of that story.

■ Though it can be difficult, it's very important for you to reveal your story to people who will understand your pain.

■ Those of us who are listening will wait to ask questions until after you are finished.

■ As you speak and as you listen, do whatever is necessary to take care of yourself.

■ Would one of you who now feels ready begin to share your memory of abuse.

> ☞*Help each speaker to tell her story with feeling. If she tells it with little affect, suggest methods to help her get in touch with her feelings, such as slowing down, taking deep breaths, and looking around at the caring faces. Encourage her to hang on to her security object, which may be a teddy bear or family picture, or suggest that she focus on any object in the room that may help her feel courageous enough to share her story.*

■ Now that you've broken your secret, I invite you to silently study the faces of the other group members. (Pause for a few moments.)

■ I encourage everyone who has been listening to share their support in any way they would like. As always, you're free to pass.

> ☞*The intensity of this process is such that we seldom hear more than two or three stories in one session.*

■ Conclude this exercise by telling those who did not tell their story that they will have an opportunity to do so in the remaining sessions.

Homework

■ During the next week, write or draw in your journal about how this group experience is healing for you.

■ Become aware of the feelings of shame you may be carrying with

©1998 Whole Person Associates 210 W Michigan Duluth MN 55802   (800) 247-6789

you as a result of the abuse. Record how this shame may be impacting you and how this group experience may be diminishing it.

Closing ritual

Again invite participants to stand in the circle that has now become a comforting, familiar, and empowering place.

- Select one word that expresses your feelings about what happened in this session. Before we leave the group, let's take a few minutes to give feedback to those who told their stories today. Our support will help them continue to heal.

After everyone who wants to has spoken, continue:

- As we close this session, remind yourself of the supportive significant others in your life by holding your wrist again as you did at the beginning of the session.

- During this week, if you feel alone, hold your wrist and recall the people who care about you and support you.

- Now, select one word that expresses your feelings for what happened in this session.

- As we raise our arms, let's say together the words we selected.

4 Breaking the Secret (part 2)

Often the process of beginning to share events of past abuse can open the floodgates of feelings for survivors. This is such a critical aspect of the entire healing process that facilitators need to offer the time required for participants to talk about the impact on their own individual healing process of breaking their secret. Therefore, two sessions dealing with this topic are often required. If necessary, repeat this session until everyone has told her story.

Goals

To continue to release feelings of fear, anger, and shame.

To normalize the feelings that may follow a survivor's sharing of her story.

To feel empowered, supported, and validated by the group.

Materials

Look at the Ceiling handout and audiotape; audiotape player; audiotape of relaxing music.

Grounding and centering

Welcome participants back to the group, encouraging them to take a few moments to center themselves and be aware of their courage in continuing their own individual healing journey.

- Revealing the secret of your abuse may be the most painful part of your healing. But through this pain, you will ultimately find peace.

- Take a few moments now to center yourself, focusing on why you are here and becoming fully aware of your courage in continuing your healing journey.

■ Put your left hand on your right wrist and once again recall the image of a mirror, filled with people who love and support you.

Examining the impact of sharing stories

It is common for survivors who share their stories to have a very difficult week troubled by additional memories of abuse and accompanying feelings of hurt and shame. Typically, they express feelings, not only of relief, but also anger, as they describe this experience to the others. Acknowledge that these feelings are normal and a part of the healing process.

Once again, it is important to allow survivors to check in and briefly report on their individual healing process. Begin this process by using the following statement:

■ Last session, several of you shared your stories with the group. Please share with us the impact this had on you during the past week.

Listen and respond to comments. When everyone who wants to has spoken, continue by affirming the speakers' courage and strength.

More stories

Ask those who shared their stories during the last session how they are now feeling. Some may continue to feel distressed, but as time goes on, they usually begin to feel less burdened, lighter, relieved, and even happy.

Distribute the handout **Look at the Ceiling.**

■ Before we continue sharing stories, we'd like to play for you a song by Peter Alsop called "Look at the Ceiling." As you listen, you can follow along on the handout.

■ The lyrics are sad and disturbing, but we hope they will help you recognize and release some of your own sad feelings.

☞*Play the song.*

Allow participants to react to and discuss the song, responding to the emotions that may be expressed.

Then continue with the process for sharing and discussion used during the previous weeks.

> ☞*Help each speaker to tell her story with feeling. If she tells it with little affect, suggest methods to help her get in touch with her feelings, such as slowing down, taking deep breaths and looking around at the caring faces. Encourage her to hang on to her security object, which may be a teddy ear or family picture, or suggest that she focus on any object in the room that may help her feel courageous enough to share her story.*

- The song we just heard may bring back memories of your own abuse. Would one of you who now feels ready, begin to share another memory with us.

- Those of us who are listening will wait to ask questions until after you are finished.

- As you speak and as you listen, do whatever is necessary to take care of yourself.

Allow participants to tell their stories, one at a time. As each person finishes her story, respond:

- Now that you've told your story, I invite you to silently study the faces of the other group members. (Pause for a few moments.)

- Those of you who recognized yourself in her story, please take turns looking at her and telling her just how you identified yourself with her abuse.

> ☞*This identification reduces the isolation and shame that abuse creates and bonds group members to each other as a sort of second (corrective) family.*

©1998 Whole Person Associates 210 W Michigan Duluth MN 55802   (800) 247-6789

Homework

By the end of this session, all of the group members will have shared at least part of their story of abuse. Encourage them to celebrate their courage.

> ☞*If this session must be repeated to give everyone a chance to tell her story, use a different homework assignment and closing ritual.*

- You should all be proud of yourselves. You showed great courage in telling your stories.

- Celebrate your continued healing by giving yourself a gift sometime during the next week as a reward for your courage.

- Come to our next session prepared to share what that gift was.

Closing ritual

Invite participants to stand in a circle. The final activity in this closing ritual creates laughter and encourages positive energy that for some survivors is a new feeling.

- We encourage you to share your thoughts about this session and the stories you heard today. (Pause for comments.)

- As we close our session, we'd like each of you, one at a time, to proclaim, "I did it." We'll all applaud your courage.

Look at the Ceiling

Look at the ceiling

The shadows are bears

I wonder what's on the TV

and Daddy's hands rub me all over

I wonder

Do leaves in the creek find their way to the sea?

Mom mashes potatoes and pours in the milk

Silently smokes cigarettes

I wish she would hug me or look at me then

I'd trade my allowance for that

Billy plays tag with me all the way home after school

Boy, he's really a brat

But we didn't do nothing

And it's not fair for Dad

To make him go home just like that

Look at the ceiling

The shadows are bears

In hurricanes where do birds hide?

Daddy's hands rub me all over

"Look at the Ceiling," page 2

I wonder

Where butterflies learn how to fly?

The county fair once had a merry-go round

I loved to watch Mom and Dad ride

We used to laugh and they used to hold hands

And neither of them used to cry

When a spider scared Little Miss Muffet away

How did she know where to run?

Oh, I'd love to sleep in the bathtub all night

And wake up clean as the sun

Look at the ceiling

The shadows are bears

Oh why do bees die when they sting

Daddy's hands rub me all over

I wonder

Where do balloons go when you cut the string?

—Peter Alsop

"Look at the Ceiling" from the following recordings: *Uniforms* audiotape, *Family Roles* audiotape, Dr. Peter Alsop's Professional Laughter Series *Songs on Sex and Sexuality* CD, and *Opening Doors* videotape. Music and lyrics by Peter Alsop—copyright 1981, 1988, and 1997, Moose School Music, BMI. Call 800-676-5480 for a catalog and for a free promotional video for booking a concert, keynote, or workshop. Peter Alsop, P.O. Box 960, Topanga, CA 90290, e-mail: peteralsop@earthlink.com.

5   The Shame that Binds

Participants are beginning to realize that "the only way out is through." In this session, they will further examine the theme of shame and how it binds survivors to the abuse and keeps them from healing.

Goals

To understand the power of shame.

To begin experiencing release from shame.

Materials

House Full of Secrets handout and audiotape by Betsy Rose; **Characteristics of a Shame-Based Family** handout.

Grounding and centering

When participants have made themselves comfortable, begin playing soothing background music and provide the following instructions:

- To help yourself become grounded and centered, place your feet flat on the floor and your hands in your lap.

- Now place one hand on the wrist of the other as a reminder that many people are supporting you (see anchoring exercise in session 3).

- Let's sit quietly for a moment as we let go of our busy day and begin to focus on the healing process within our group.

Introduce the song on audiotape, "House Full of Secrets" by Betsy Rose and distribute the words of the song as a handout.

- We're going to listen to a song written by Betsy Rose, "House Full of Secrets." The song describes a survivor's experience in her family.

©1998 Whole Person Associates 210 W Michigan Duluth MN 55802   (800) 247-6789

☞*This song often evokes strong emotions from participants. Take time to process them.*

Releasing the shame

Distribute the handout **Characteristics of a Shame-Based Family**.

Using some of the following questions and comments, encourage discussion:

- Do any of the characteristics on this list remind you of your childhood family? Which ones?

- Which characteristic caused you the most pain? Why?

- Which characteristic caused you to feel ashamed of yourself instead of your abuser?

- Are you still living out any of these characteristics in your own home?

Conclude this part of the session by reminding participants:

- You are not alone. Many people live throughout their childhood in families that control members by making them feel ashamed of their thoughts, feelings, and behaviors.

- You have shown courage in facing and addressing your feelings of shame.

- When you face those feelings and recognize where they came from, you can begin to discard them and move on towards healing.

Homework

Introduce the homework assignment for the week, which is built on the handout used at the beginning of this session.

- This coming week, review the handouts we gave you today, **House Full of Secrets and Characteristics of a Shame-Based Family**.

- After you reflect on these materials and today's discussion, imagine what might be a metaphor for your shame, then a metaphor for releasing it.

- Then select a way of expressing that metaphor by choosing an object, drawing a picture, or writing about it.

  ☞Be prepared to offer an example. One survivor drew a picture of shame as fire burning within her body and then drew another picture of group members pouring cool water out of a beautiful pitcher onto the flames.

Closing ritual

Form a circle and allow time for sharing the feelings that telling stories releases. Give an opportunity for participants to express hurt and anger, and offer support, such as hugs. Before opening the circle, check that everyone is okay and able to drive home.

©1998 Whole Person Associates 210 W Michigan Duluth MN 55802   (800) 247-6789

House Full of Secrets

Words and music by Betsy Rose

It is not so much the direct abuse that leaves lasting wounds on us, but the secrets we continue to keep long after childhood days are gone.

Chorus:
In the house full of secrets, with curtains of doubt
You may run away early or stay much too long
But you're trying to get out
And it clings to your body, your voice and your dreams
'Til you find that you're still keeping secrets
And you never feel clean

They smile when they're angry, they joke when they're sad
There are sudden explosions and good times gone bad
And you're caught in the crossfire like a kite in a storm
And you learn how to change with their weather
But you never feel warm

And they hide it in bottles they hide it in food
In jovial teasing and sudden dark moods
And public opinion becomes God on the throne
And children learn early to show a good face
And keep secrets alone

Chorus:
In the house full of secrets, with curtains of doubt
You may run away early or stay much too long
But you're trying to get out
And it clings to your habits like cobwebs and dust
'Til you find that you're still keeping secrets
From the ones that you love

"House Full of Secrets," page 2

And maybe you loved them and you wanted to please
So you joined in the secrets you caught the disease
You polished the doorknob didn't turn them too hard
Didn't poke where you might not be wanted
Oh you stayed in the yard

Or maybe you learned hatred all bottled and sealed
Like a knife cutting out what you can't bear to feel
And you wish you were softer that the door would swing wide
But your anger's too narrow
And the path of forgiveness too wide

Chorus:
For the house full of secrets, with curtains of doubt
You may run away early or stay much too long
But you're trying to get out
And it fogs up the window it muddies your view
'Til you find that you're still keeping secrets—even from you

There's a story you heard as a child of a puppet who tried to get free
When he ran from his father he fell into bad company
So you learned that a life without strings is a dangerous deal
But you're haunted by stories with endings where puppets get real

Tell my sisters and my brothers who carry this load
We can't run away but we have to leave home
I'm spilling my secrets my back's to the wall
I'm saving my own skin
Let the house of cards fall

"House Full of Secrets," page 3

And may the house that I build with my lover and my friends
Have windows flung open to sunlight and wind
May the moments of darkness not tear us apart
And may the children speak freely the secrets
And the dreams of their hearts

Leave the house full of secrets!
Draw the curtains of doubt
If you ran away early, or stayed much too long—
You've time to get out
No promise of sunshine, no slick guarantees
You may not be happy or holy or sweet
But by God you'll be free
From your house full of secrets!

© 1987 Betsy Rose, available from Paper Crane Music, P.O.
Box 9538, Berkely, CA 94709, 888-267-4833 (pin #8340)

Characteristics of a Shame-Based Family

Feelings are denied, avoided, discounted, and suppressed.

Family secrets are preserved at all cost.

Control is maintained by fear and secrecy.

Perfection is expected, mistakes are not allowed.

Blame is freely placed whenever anything goes wrong.

Love is conditional.

The "no-talk" rule prohibits the expression of feelings, needs, or wants.

Trusting no one assures that you will never be disappointed.

6 The Child Within

The next two sessions focus on helping survivors to experience the part of themselves that they typically repressed in order to survive their childhood. These sessions are critical to the healing process. They allow survivors to recover the part of themselves that, because of the abuse they suffered, never had an opportunity to grow and flourish. We refer to this part as the "child within." This is the part of all human beings that allows them to laugh, to cry, to feel joy, anxiety, love, and peace. For healing to occur, survivors need to be given explicit permission to feel their feelings and express them. Expressing within the group what was difficult to express as an abused child will allow survivors to welcome feelings into their daily lives.

Goals

To recognize the child within and allow it to come forth.

To feel and express emotions of joy, sadness, and anger.

Materials

Audiotape player; audiotape with relaxing music, audiotape containing background music plus ocean sounds; paper, pencils, and markers or crayons.

Grounding and centering

When participants have all made themselves comfortable, welcome them, then begin playing soothing background music. Begin with the usual grounding and centering routine, then continue with the deep breathing script.

■ To help yourself become grounded and centered, place your feet flat on the floor and your hands in your lap.

■ As you sit quietly and relax, place one hand on the wrist of the other as a reminder that many people are supporting you.

Deep breathing script

Breathing deeply now, begin to let go of your busy day and focus on the healing process within our group . . .

Close your eyes now and focus on your breathing . . . breathe in and feel the air fill your lungs . . . all the way to the bottom . . . Now breathe out and let that air flow out of your lungs . . . Breathe in . . . breathe out . . .

Breathe in, relaxing all the muscles in your back, neck, and shoulders . . . breathe out, relaxing your chest and abdomen . . .

Breathe in quiet and peace . . .

Breathe out stress and tension . . .

Breathe in . . . breathe out . . . (pause for 1 minute)

Continue to breathe slowly and deeply . . . When you are ready, open your eyes and look around at the people who are here, ready to support you as you heal.

Shame metaphors

As participants share their metaphors for shame, reach for the feelings of anger that often are stirred up in this exercise and normalize those feelings.

■ Last session, we asked you to select a metaphor for the shame you felt as a child and find some way to share that metaphor with the group.

■ Some of you may have written or drawn your metaphor, others may have brought along an object that demonstrates what it felt like to bear this burden of shame.

©1998 Whole Person Associates 210 W Michigan Duluth MN 55802   (800) 247-6789

- Who will begin by showing her metaphor and explaining the meaning it has for her?

As participants describe their metaphors, they can be encouraged to express their feelings by asking questions about their inner child. This will also serve as a bridge to the work of the rest of the session:

- What would the little child who is feeling this shame like to say?

- What does that child want to do with the shame?

Meeting the child within

To help participants recognize their inner child, use the following relaxation and imagery scripts. Distribute writing and drawing materials before you begin.

- Today you will have a chance to meet and talk with your inner child. We'll begin with a few minutes of physical relaxation that will prepare you for an imaginary journey.

  ☞Read the script slowly, pausing briefly between phrases and for a longer time between sentences and paragraphs. When you give an instruction, be sure to give participants plenty of time to complete the action before you move on.

  Give yourself permission to relax by sitting with your back supported and allow yourself to ground by putting both feet flat on the floor . . . As a way to turn inward, you may want to put your hands in your lap and let your chin rest on your chest . . .

  When you feel your eyelids growing heavy, allow your eyes to close . . . a nice way to close out the outside world and feel even more grounded . . . focus inward and relax . . .

  Give yourself permission to observe any sounds around you and know you can let them be . . .

  Scan your body for tension . . . help it to be comfortable and relaxed . . .

Tune in now to your breathing . . . Notice your own rhythm and how its regularity can soothe you . . . Every once in a while you may wish to take a deep cleansing breath . . . inhaling through your nose and exhaling slowly through your mouth . . . Notice the moment of inner peace at the top of the in-breath before you exhale . . .

This time . . . as you exhale . . . blow out as though you're making a candle flame flicker with your breath . . . long, slow exhale without blowing out the flame . . . again . . . and again.

> ☞*While participants continue their deep, slow breathing, begin playing softly an audiotape that includes sounds of the ocean; then continue with the imagery script.*

Notice your surroundings as you hear the ocean waves . . . It is a warm, summer day . . . The birds fly through the air and dive into the water . . . Feel the sun on your body and the sand between your toes . . . a slight breeze playing with your hair as you enjoy walking along the water's edge . . . taste the salt in the air . . .

It is good to be alone for now . . . You feel at peace with yourself, a feeling that comes to you more and more these days as you continue to heal and grow . . .

Look down the beach now toward the cliffs in the distance . . . As you continue your walk, you notice a small child just ahead playing with a pail and shovel in the sand . . . Her head is down and she seems intent on what she's doing . . . As you get closer, study her . . . Who does she look like? . . . What is the expression on her face? . . . How old is she? . . . What is she wearing and how does her hair look? . . . Notice as much as you can about her . . .

She sees you now . . . How does she react? . . . What do you do? . . . Spend some time with her . . . (longer pause)

It is time to leave the beach now . . . The sun is setting; you feel a slight chill in the air and the sand is cooling under your feet . . .

Take a moment to think about what you want to take home from this experience . . .

☞*Gradually reduce the music's volume.*

Turn away from the water now and make your way back along the way you came . . . Notice now your body in the present, your feet on the ground, the silence after the waves, your breathing as you prepare to tune into the present . . .

And now take a deep cleansing breath, open your eyes,, then focus, reach for paper and pencil or crayons; and write or draw about your experience . . .

Encourage the discussion of what this guided imagery evoked for each survivor and ask them to share what they drew or wrote. It is important to focus on the significance of their connection to this child.

Homework

For participants to become familiar with the concept of nurturing their inner child, they need to take time exploring their own sense of their child within.

- During the next week, think more about the child within you.

- Find pictures of yourself as a child.

- Explore what children are like by going to a playground, school, or shopping mall, or observe your own children as they play.

- Draw and write about the lives of children.

- If you didn't have a special doll when you were a child, you may want to buy one now.

- Most important, take time to feel the little girl within yourself. Take time to discover how she is feeling about your healing process.

- Bring what you discover to next week's session.

Closing ritual

Invite participants to form a circle.

■ As a first step in exploring the child within you, I invite you share with the group one thing you know for sure about that child.

7   Exploring Repressed Feelings

This session continues with the theme of the child within. Most survivors have learned to repress their feelings in order to protect themselves from hurt and pain. It is the child within who holds those feelings, waiting for permission to express them.

Goals

To learn more about the child within.

To encourage survivors to risk expressing their feelings.

Materials

Audiotape player; audiotape with relaxing music; audiotape of "How Could Anyone" by Libby Roderick; **How Could Anyone** handout; paper; clipboards; pens and crayons.

Grounding and centering

When participants have all made themselves comfortable, welcome them, then begin playing soothing background music and provide the following instructions:

- To help yourself become grounded and centered, place your feet flat on the floor and your hands in your lap.

- Now place one hand on the wrist of the other as a reminder that many people are supporting you.

- Remain quiet for a few moments as you bring yourself into the present with this group, leaving behind your busy daily schedule.

Exploring participants' discovery of the child within

To encourage participants to continue exploring the child within themselves, ask them to share what they discovered the previous week. This process produces laughter, tears, and the expression of many feelings, which you will want to normalize.

- This past week, you were asked to explore and learn more about the child within you.

- Let's hear what you discovered.

- If you brought along photos or objects, please share them with the group.

  > ☞*Often as survivors share pictures of themselves as children, they become more aware of all children's vulnerability and especially their own vulnerability at the time of the abuse. Feelings of sadness and loss emerge. This often is a healing moment.*

Alternate hand dialogue

Soft background music can be played during the following activity. The song by Libby Roderick "How Could Anyone" is our favorite. If you use that song, distribute the **How Could Anyone** handout as they listen.

Distribute paper, a clipboard, a pen and a crayon to each participant and give the following instructions.

- I invite you to dialogue with the little girl inside of you.

- Using a pen in your dominant hand (the one you usually write with), write questions to her from the adult in you, then pick up your crayon with your nondominant hand and let the little girl in you respond to the questions.

If participants have trouble getting started, suggest questions such as:

- Are you ashamed of what happened?

- Are you angry at me?

- What do you need from me?

- How can I make it better now?

Discussion can be brief. The process, itself, is more useful and important than sharing with group members.

> ☞Occasionally, survivors will say that they feel foolish doing this exercise. Reassure them that this is an important exercise in the healing process and has had remarkable success with many other survivors. Some say that they experienced feelings for the first time during this exercise. Emotions can be strong and often for the first time a strong bond is created between the survivor and their child within.

Homework

Encourage participants to continue this kind of dialoguing at home during the week.

- During this next week, discover more about your inner child by continuing a dialogue with her.

- If it feels safe to do so, begin sharing your feelings and what you are learning about yourself with significant others in your life.

- You are talking about these issues within our group, but it's important also to talk with other people who are important to you.

Closing ritual

Ask participants to join in the closing circle, carrying their dialogues with them.

- Place the dialogue with your inner child in the center of our circle for everyone to see.

©1998 Whole Person Associates 210 W Michigan Duluth MN 55802   (800) 247-6789

■ As you look at the childlike handwriting, take turns saying something nurturing to your own child within or to the child within of others in our group.

How Could Anyone

Words and music by Libby Roderick

How could anyone ever tell you
You were anything less than beautiful?
How could anyone ever tell you
You were less than whole?
How could anyone fail to notice
That your loving is a miracle?
How deeply you're connected to my soul.

How Could Anyone
Words and music by Libby Roderick,
© 1988 Libby Roderick Music
From the recording *If You See a Dream*
Available through Turtle Island Records
P.O. Box 203294, Anchorage, AK 99520-3294
907-278-6817

8   Releasing Anger

In this session, survivors are helped to see that the anger that they have internalized (often felt as rage) is justified. Facilitators support their need to release this anger, suggest safe ways to do this, and provide boundaries so survivors can maintain a sense of control during this process.

Goals

Learn how to release anger safely.

Understand that anger may be justified and appropriate.

Practice expressing anger.

Materials

Paper and pens; clipboards; large outline drawing of a childlike figure; easel paper and markers; **Confrontation: An Important Part of Healing** handout; **Prepare to Confront your Abuser** worksheet; wastebasket.

Grounding and centering

When participants have all made themselves comfortable, welcome them, then provide the following instructions:

- To help yourself become grounded and centered, place your feet flat on the floor and your hands in your lap.

- Now place one hand on the wrist of the other as a reminder that many people are supporting you.

- Remain quiet for a few moments as you bring yourself into the present with this group, leaving behind your busy daily schedule. (pause)

Drawing out the anger

> ☞*This exercise allows survivors to express anger as a group. It also prepares them for the main theme of this session which is releasing their anger at the abuser.*

Ask participants to share any experiences with their inner child:

- For a few moments, close your eyes and again imagine the child you once were.

- Now open your eyes and share with the group any experiences you had with your child since the last session.

Tape to the wall a large outline drawing of a childlike figure, then begin the process of encouraging participants to identify and describe their pain.

- On the wall, I have taped a drawing of a child's figure.

- On this drawing, I'd like each of you to mark the place where you feel the pain of being abused as a child.

After each participant has marked the drawing, continue:

- As you look at the drawing of this wounded child and feel her pain, describe for the group what it is like for you to remember this abuse.

After everyone has responded, you should feel free and encouraged to express your own anger at the abuse represented by this drawing.

Unsent letter to abuser

Distribute paper, pens, and clipboards and give the following instructions, inviting each participant to write an angry letter to her abuser:

- You will have the opportunity now to write a letter to your abuser, a letter that will never be mailed.

- There is no need to worry about punctuation, spelling, or neatness during this exercise.

■ You will have 5 minutes to write your letter. Please begin writing when we tell you to start and don't stop writing until time is up.

    ☞*This process encourages a continuous flow of feeling and allows for the intensity to build yet draws boundaries around the activity.*

■ Begin now. (Allow 5 minutes for this process).

Continue by encouraging discussion of and normalizing the intense feelings, such as anxiety, guilt, and fear, that are often experienced during the letter writing process.

For some survivors, this may be the first time that they have given themselves permission to release their anger. You may want to provide some psycho-education about anger:

■ Anger is a natural human feeling that everyone experiences.

■ It can be a source of energy.

■ However, it needs to be released in safe ways.

Brainstorm some of the safe ways in which anger can be released, writing them on the easel paper. If the following ideas are not mentioned, you could add them to the list along with your own favorite anger release activities:

■ toss darts

■ hurl nerf balls

■ pound pillows

■ throw ice cubes into a bathtub

Review goals

Remind participants that they are more than halfway through this group experience and that it is time to review the goals they originally established. After having dealt with the highly intense release of anger, this is a good time to support and reassure group members that they are making progress in their healing.

> ☞*Make sure that participants' goal sheets (written during session 1) are posted.*

■ We are now more than half way through our experience together.

■ During our first session together, each of you listed your goals. You have been working very hard, and it's time to look at how many of those goals you have already accomplished.

■ Review your list and after each goal, rank on a scale of 1 to 10 how far along you are toward the accomplishment of that goal.

■ If necessary, add to or revise your list in response to what you have learned about yourself and the healing process.

> ☞*Pay close attention to this process and help participants retain appropriate and realistic healing goals. Allow them to renegotiate their goals if necessary.*

Homework

Distribute the **Confrontation: An Important Part of Healing** and **Prepare to Confront Your Abuser** handouts, then give the following instructions for homework:

■ In our next session, we will explore the theme of confrontation.

■ The **Confrontation: An Important Part of Healing** handout provides information about healthy confrontation. Please read and think about it.

■ The **Prepare to Confront Your Abuser** worksheet gives you the opportunity to consider and state your feelings about confrontation and to begin planning how you might confront your abuser. Please complete the worksheet and bring it to next week's session.

Closing ritual

Ask participants to gather in a circle, bringing with them the letter they wrote. Place a wastebasket in the center of the circle. Offer words of support and encouragement.

■ Again this week, you have shown great courage by talking about the abuse you suffered and by beginning the process of confronting your abuser.

■ We are proud of the progress you are making toward meeting your goals, and we hope you are too.

■ As we conclude today's session, take the letter you wrote to your abuser, crush it into a ball, and throw it into this wastebasket. Let that action symbolize for you that you can feel your anger, express your anger, and then let go of your anger.

☞*Make sure participants know how you will dispose of the letters in a way that maintains confidentiality.*

Confrontation: An Important Part of Healing

Prepare yourself

- You need to be emotionally prepared to significantly change your relationship with your abuser and, if necessary, to lose it.

- You need to have shifted your beliefs and accept that you are NOT responsible for the abuse.

- You need to have a strong support system.

- You need to PRACTICE, PRACTICE, PRACTICE!!

Remember

- Confrontation is not to punish, retaliate, or put down your abuser.

- Confrontation is not to dump your anger on your abuser.

- Confrontation is not to get something back from your abuser.

- Confrontation is to face your fear.

- Confrontation is to tell the truth.

- Confrontation is to determine the type of relationship you can have in the future.

Hold your abuser accountable for

- A full acknowledgment of what happened.

- An apology.

- Their full acceptance of responsibility for what happened.

- Their willingness to make reparations.

Prepare to Confront Your Abuser

- When I hear the word "confrontation" the picture that comes to my mind is . . .

- When I think of confronting my abuser, I feel . . .

- To prepare to confront my abuser, I would need . . .

- When I confront my abuser, I hope that . . .

9   Imagining Confrontation

In the previous sessions, participants experienced the process of finding the child within, communicating with her, and making her feel as safe as possible. They now have an opportunity to express anger toward their abuser in a healthy way. Participants are now ready to explore the theme of confronting their abuser.

Exploring confrontation in a group can be a powerful healing experience. Therefore, even though participants may have already confronted their abuser on their own or have decided they will never confront their abuser, encourage them to participate fully in this session.

Goals

To experience through a visualization some of the feelings connected with confrontation.

To practice confrontation through a letter-writing exercise.

Materials

Audiotape player; audiotape of lullabies; audiotape suitable for jungle visualization; paper, pens, and crayons.

Grounding and centering

When participants have all made themselves comfortable, welcome them; distribute paper, pens, and crayons; begin playing softly an audiotape of lullabies; then provide the following instructions:

- To help yourself become grounded and centered, place your feet flat on the floor and your hands in your lap.

- Now place one hand on the wrist of the other as a reminder that many people are supporting you.

■ Remain quiet for a few moments as you listen to the lullabies and reflect on your inner child.

Preparing the child within

By listening to survivors' responses to some of the questions that follow, assess how each woman is continuing to nurture herself in her daily life. Remind participants how important it is to stay in contact with the child within, who may have been hiding for years. This discussion will prepare participants for the exercise on confrontation.

■ How do you make that little girl inside of you feel safe?

■ How do you reassure her that it is okay to express feelings?

■ How do you bring her out to play?

■ Can you comfort her when she feels anxious or fearful?

Confrontation in imagination

Introduce the concept of confrontation in imagination:

■ You can prepare to confront your abuser by imagining how you might do this.

■ Even if you never confront your abuser in reality, it's valuable for you to imagine the situation.

■ To prepare for this real or imaginary confrontation, we will begin with a few minutes of relaxation then continue by visualizing a jungle scene.

Deep breathing script

Sit quietly and relax, breathing deeply as you let go of your busy day and begin to focus on the healing process within our group . . .

Close your eyes now and focus on your breathing . . . breathe in and feel the air fill your lungs . . . all the way to the bottom . . . Now breathe out and let that air flow out of your lungs . . . Breathe in . . . breathe out . . .

Breathe in, relaxing all the muscles in your back, neck, and shoulders . . . breathe out, relaxing your chest and abdomen . . .

Breathe in quiet and peace . . .

Breathe out stress and tension . . .

Breathe in . . . breathe out . . . (pause for 1 minute)

Continue to breathe slowly and deeply . . .

Jungle confrontation script

Continue with the following visualization which will help survivors become aware of their feelings about confronting their abusers. Begin playing an audiotape with music appropriate to a jungle scene. Change your tone of voice to suggest tension rather than relaxation and allow that tension to increase. Speak more rapidly, but leave time where indicated for participants to visualize what you are describing.

You are in a thick jungle with lots of vines, trees, and ground cover . . . walking on a path which is barely visible . . . You are aware of the heat . . . the sound of birds . . . and bugs . . . as well as the feel of the sun as it peaks through the thick foliage every once in a while . . .

You may feel yourself begin to sweat as you struggle with finding the path and staying on it . . . Your heart may begin to beat a little faster as you move along, but even in your discomfort you are determined and focused on continuing your journey to get out of the jungle . . .

Your fear suddenly increases as you look down the path you're on and see a tiger staring at you . . . He is poised and alert but not yet sure of who you are or what he should do. . . Watch the tiger . . . observe your own reactions . . .

You know that in order to continue your journey, you must deal with this tiger . . . think it through . . . and decide what to do . . .

*Once you have decided the best way for you to handle this situation . . .
act on your decision . . . Visualize your action and its results . . .*

*And now, what has happened? . . . How do you feel? . . . Where is the
tiger? . . . Can you see your way clear to continue your journey? . . .*

*Move now through the rest of the jungle with a new speed and sense of
freedom until you once again emerge from the jungle and return to the
present . . .*

*Notice your body's reaction to the present . . . feel the floor . . . notice
your breathing . . . release any tension with deep soothing breaths . . .
Return again to the music and the physical relaxation you have learned
to enjoy . . .*

Now open your eyes . . . focus and return to the present . . .

- Reach for paper and a pen or crayons and draw or write about this
  experience.

Discussion of feelings about confrontation

After the writing and drawing is completed, lead a discussion of
participants' responses to the visualization and to their homework
assignment. Reactions to these experiences may vary. Discussion
allows group members to learn that they can gather support from
and offer support to each other as they face the very difficult issue
of confrontation.

Encourage participants who have already confronted their abuser
to share their experiences.

Point out the need for careful preparation and rehearsal before any
actual confrontation takes place.

> ☞*It has been our experience that survivors who have con-
> fronted their abusers without preparation have not had an
> empowering experience; therefore this session is significant
> even for them.*

Homework

Invite participants to prepare three letters for the next session. Help participants understand that writing letters that will never be sent is a useful, safe way for them to explore confrontation, as well as a method they can use as they work through any other issues in life. The assignment includes:

1. A letter that states everything she would want to say to her abuser.

2. A letter from her abuser that states what she imagines her abuser would say in response to her letter.

3. A letter from her abuser that states what she hopes her abuser would say in response to her letter.

Closing ritual

Invite participants to gather in the closing circle and make some of the following comments:

- Even thinking about confronting your abuser can be difficult, especially for your inner child. But writing these three letters is an important part of your healing process.

- How do you plan to take care of your little girl as you write your three letters?

    ☞*Encourage participants to use all they are learning from each other to take care of themselves as they face their fears of confrontation.*

10 Practicing Confrontation

Through role play, each participant has the opportunity to rehearse what she would say and do if she were to confront her abuser in real life. Supported by the group, survivors are empowered to make healthy choices concerning confrontation of their abuser.

Goals

To practice confronting the abuser.

To begin letting go of the abuse.

To begin preparing for the end of the group experience.

Materials

Two extra chairs.

Grounding and centering

When participants have all made themselves comfortable, welcome them, then provide the following instructions:

- To help yourself become grounded and centered, place your feet flat on the floor and your hands in your lap.

- Now place one hand on the wrist of the other as a reminder that many people are supporting you.

- Remain quiet for a few moments as you explore in your mind's eye how your healing journey has been unfolding.

Monitoring the healing journey

To help participants continue to reflect on their healing journey, use some of the following questions and comments:

- This past week, were you able to balance the three letter writing exercises with the nurturing of yourself?

- How did you do this?

Acknowledge and support each participant's efforts and successes. It's important that this warm-up time is positive and empowering.

Empty chair role play

In this exercise, participants will practice confronting their abuser, who they imagine is sitting in the empty chair. Because this can be a potentially frightening experience, no one in the group, including the facilitators, should play the part of the abuser.

Place two chairs, facing each other, in the center of the group and provide the following instructions:

- Today, each of you will have the opportunity for an imaginary confrontation with your abuser. As always, you may choose not to participate if you don't feel ready.

- You will sit in one chair and imagine that your abuser is sitting in the other chair.

- After you are seated, close your eyes and take a few deep breaths.

- When you are ready, open your eyes, face the empty chair, and begin reading the first letter that you wrote this week, the one that explains what you have experienced as a result of the abuse.

      During this process normalize feelings of anxiety, anger, and fear and encourage support from the group.

After the first letter is read, other participants are asked to respond as they would imagine the abuser might respond.

- What might this abuser say in response to the confrontation?

- Respond from the abuser's perspective, presenting portions from your second letter.

After each participant who is willing has a chance to practice confronting her abuser, remove the chairs and allow participants to once again ground and center themselves with a few minutes of deep breathing.

Deep breathing script

Sit quietly and relax, breathing deeply as you let go of the tension of the role play and again focus on the healing process within our group . . .

Close your eyes now and focus on your breathing . . . breathe in and feel the air fill your lungs . . . all the way to the bottom . . . Now breathe out and let that air flow out of your lungs . . . Breathe in . . . breathe out . . .

Breathe in, relaxing all the muscles in your back, neck, and shoulders . . . breathe out, relaxing your chest and abdomen

Breathe in quiet and peace . . .

Breathe out stress and tension . . .

Breathe in . . . breathe out . . . (pause for 1 minute)

Continue to breathe slowly and deeply . . .

The final step in this process is for participants to read aloud their third letters.

■ The third letter you wrote this week is one in which your abuser acknowledges the abuse and asks your forgiveness.

■ You may now take turns reading those letters. Let's withhold comment until all the letters have been read.

  ☞*This is often an intense and powerful exercise for the participants. Accept and normalize feelings of sadness and anger.*

Homework

The emotions of sadness that surface during the reading of these "ideal letters" provide a natural bridge to introduce the next session's theme of grief and loss.

- We now approach a critical step in your healing process, letting go of the abuse.

- It is also time to prepare for letting go of this group experience as there are only two sessions left.

- Over the course of the next week, begin the process of letting go by writing a list of all that you have lost as a result of your abuse. Keep adding to the list throughout the week.

Closing ritual

After participants gather in the closing circle, place an empty chair in the center of the group, then lead a closing discussion using some of the following questions:

- Please share some of your thoughts about today's session?

- How do you feel about the abuser's chair being in the center of our circle?

- What would you like to do with the chair before you leave for home?

    ☞*Typically, group members want to kick the chair, hit it, swear at it, etc. Acknowledge these feelings before presenting the following invitation:*

- Together, let's pick up this chair and remove it from the center of our circle and from the center of our lives.

After triumphantly removing the chair from the circle, gather the group and close with a group hug and cheer.

11 Grieving Losses

The theme of grief and loss is important in the healing process. We have found that many abuse survivors resist feeling sadness and loss. When these feelings come to the surface and are dealt with, survivors can then let go of their experience of abuse and grow, develop, and thrive.

Goals

To acknowledge and grieve losses.

To explore ways to retrieve some of these losses.

To reflect on the continuing healing journey.

To begin preparing for the final session together.

Materials

Paper and pencils; easel pad and markers; audiotape player; audiotape of relaxing music.

Grounding and centering

When participants have all made themselves comfortable, welcome them, then provide the following instructions:

- To help yourself become grounded and centered, place your feet flat on the floor and your hands in your lap.

- Now place one hand on the wrist of the other as a reminder that many people are supporting you.

- Remain quiet for a few moments as you explore in your mind's eye how your healing journey has been unfolding.

Exploring emptiness

As a result of the last session on confrontation of their abuser, it is not unusual for group participants to experience a sense of emptiness.

Continue the grounding and centering process by asking participants to share with the group how they are feeling about this part of their healing process. Accept and normalize feelings of sadness, loss, and emptiness.

Retrieving losses

After plenty of time and opportunity has been provided for the expression of feelings, continue by distributing paper and pencils and asking participants to reflect on their losses.

- Women who were abused as children have lost many things.

- On the paper we provided, make a list of the losses you experienced due to your abuse.

When participants have completed their lists, ask them to call out their losses as you make a group list on the easel paper.

> ☞*Participants are often overwhelmed when they view such a diverse list. Encourage them to express their feelings of sadness.*

After each participant has had an opportunity to express their losses, introduce the theme of survivors becoming strong at the broken places.

- When a broken bone heals, it is often stronger at the point of the break than anywhere else.

- You, too, have broken places because of your abuse.

- But you are now healing and are becoming strong at those broken places.

- Look at your own list and the list on the board. What can you retrieve from the losses you experienced? How can you become strong again?

☞*Participants often talk about taking back their bodies, regaining their ability to express feelings, and retrieving their femininity and even their virginity.*

Continue by inviting participants to brainstorm ways to recover some of these losses. Encourage them to offer ideas to each other. This discussion is usually lively and shows the strong support these survivors have developed for each other.

☞*One woman asked her husband to make love to her as though she was a virgin. Another had her mate buy her a wrist corsage because she wasn't allowed to go to her high school prom. One survivor bought body lotion and massaged her own body as a healing experience.*

Homework

In preparation for the homework assignment, lead a brief visualization, preceding it with a relaxation exercise. Soft music can be played.

Sit quietly and relax, breathing deeply as you again focus on the healing process within our group . . .

Close your eyes now and focus on your breathing . . . breathe in and feel the air fill your lungs . . . all the way to the bottom . . . Now breathe out and let that air flow out of your lungs . . . Breathe in . . . breathe out . . .

Breathe in, relaxing all the muscles in your back, neck, and shoulders . . . breathe out, relaxing your chest and abdomen

Breathe in quiet and peace . . .

Breathe out stress and tension . . .

Breathe in . . . breathe out . . . (pause for 1 minute)

Continue to breathe slowly and deeply . . .

You are walking slowly along a path through a sunny meadow . . . a healing path . . . Feel the comforting warmth of the sun on your back . . . Notice how calm and relaxed you feel.

Turn very slowly and look behind you . . . You can see the journey you have traveled . . . from the very first steps until today.

Notice the bumps in the road . . . this was not an easy journey . . . Perhaps you made some detours along the way . . . or you may have stumbled and wondered if you could continue.

You have made great progress and you feel proud of yourself.

Now turn again and look down the path that extends before you . . . Where do you need to travel next on your healing journey? What do you need to do? . . .

You feel positive and confident about your next steps, ready to move ahead toward complete healing.

When you are ready, open your eyes and find yourself in the present, in the middle of your journey.

Homework

- During this week, continue to reflect on your healing journey. Find a creative and visual way to represent your healing path and bring that representation to the next session.

  ☞*Survivors we have worked with have brought poetry, posterboard maps, cartoons, and collages. It is important to encourage survivors to tap their natural creativity and anchor in this visual way their own sense of their healing journey.*

Closing ritual

Gather participants in a circle for the closing ritual and offer them an opportunity to express empathy for each other's losses.

> ☞*The metaphor of a wake might be helpful: good friends gathering to offer sympathy to each other.*

Continue by preparing participants for the final session.

> ☞*In our experience, a two-week break before the final session helps participants prepare for it.*

- Our next session will be the last meeting for our group.

- Before the session, consider how you might want to express to others in our group your gratitude for their support. If you would like to, you might bring a small gift for each person in the group.

- Think also about how you may want to say good-bye to each other.

12 Bittersweet Endings

The last session of this group for survivors is designed to provide an opportunity to "do endings" in a different way than perhaps they have had the opportunity to do before.

To give participants time to work on their individual healing goals and to prepare to say good-bye to the group, the session is deliberately delayed for two weeks after the eleventh session.

Goals

To celebrate progress made toward goals.

To say good-bye to others in the group and to the facilitators.

To seek ongoing support from therapists and significant others.

Materials

A sprig of bittersweet (either natural or made from materials in a craft store); **Circle of Light** handout; audiotape of "Circle of Light"; **Invitation to Session for Significant Others** letter; gifts for each participant from the facilitators (select a gift for each participant, depending on her needs. Consider items such as seashells, handmade pins, bubble bath, or cards).

Grounding and centering

When participants have all made themselves comfortable, welcome them, then provide the following instructions:

- To help yourself become grounded and centered, place your feet flat on the floor and your hands in your lap.

- Now place one hand on the wrist of the other as a reminder that many people, including all the members of this group, are supporting you.

- Remain quiet for a few moments as you regain the feeling of calm and peace that you have felt in the past weeks.

- You can recall that feeling at any time by sitting quietly and placing your hand on your wrist.

Show and tell

Encourage participants to talk about the strides they have taken along their healing path and to show the visual representations of their journeys that they prepared as part of their homework.

☞*It is important to use this exercise as an opportunity to affirm the progress of each survivor.*

Bittersweet endings

After each participant has shared her current progress, the following exercise is introduced as a way to end this group experience.

- I have in my hand a sprig of bittersweet, a reminder of how bitter and how sweet this final session of our group is.

- Bitter, because endings are always sad.

- Sweet, because you have shown such courage and made such progress in your healing journey.

- I'm going to pass the bittersweet around. When it comes to you, share with us your feelings about ending this group, what you will be leaving behind and what you will be taking with you—the bitter and the sweet.

Conclude this exercise by making the following comments:

- You are connected to the many other survivors who have participated in this healing journey. They, too, found it bittersweet to leave the group.

©1998 Whole Person Associates 210 W Michigan Duluth MN 55802   (800) 247-6789

- And you are also connected to the many women who are still keeping the secret of their abuse. You can give them the courage to begin their journey.

Sharing

As homework, each participant was invited to bring to this last session something that would symbolize the meaning that this group experience has had for her. Give them time to share their poems, artwork, and music with each other.

Giving

If participants brought gifts for each other, allow them to share them. The simple act of giving gifts to each other creates a powerful healing experience.

Planning for support

Encourage participants to plan for continued support. You may want to suggest that they:

- Contact their individual therapists.

- Reconnect with significant others and share their experiences along with their need for support. This is particularly important if they will be confronting their abuser or parents who did not protect them from abuse.

- Exchange phone numbers with others in the group.

Closing ritual

Gather participants in the final closing circle and encourage them to connect physically by holding hands or placing their arms around each others' shoulders.

Play the song "Circle of Light" by Betsy Rose. Because this is an upbeat, lighthearted song, tears of sadness may turn into laughter, illustrating again the bittersweet nature of good-byes.

Before participants leave

Distribute the **Circle of Light** handout.

Offer participants the opportunity to take individual goal sheets that have been posted since session 2 home with them.

Distribute the letters inviting significant others (partners, siblings, close friends, etc.) to a one-session group and provide the following information:

- This letter is an invitation that you may give to significant people in your life. It invites them to attend a one-session group meeting in which we will describe the process of healing that survivors often go through. This information can help people understand the process and be supportive.

- The session is voluntary, and it's up to you whether you want to share the letter. The session will be educational rather than therapeutic. You and other survivors won't be present, but your confidentiality will be respected.

Circle of Light

Words and music by Betsy Rose

In a circle of fire
In a circle of light
Come together, Come to sing, Come to this night
Come on sisters, Come on brothers
Climb aboard, hang on tight
We're taking pride in a circle of light

In a circle of light
In a circle of peace
Leave your troubles at the door and be relieved
Every heart is hungry-come on welcome to the feast of harmony
In a circle of peace

In a circle of peace
In a circle of friends
You can lay your burden down and start again
No more whispering in the shadows
Come on, join the angels' band
And lend a hand in the circle of friends

In a circle of friends
In a circle of song
Every frog, every sparrow sing along

"Circle of Light," page 2

If they told you to be silent

You can show them they were wrong

And it will make you strong

In a circle of song

In a circle of song

In a circle of fire

Catch the spark that set you blazing with desire

Every voice can move a mountain

Every breath can be a choir

And we'll conspire

In a circle of fire

In a circle of fire

In a circle of light

Come together, come to sing, come to this night

Let it echo in the valley

Let it ring from the mountain height

We're taken flight

In a circle of light

Going to see things right

In a circle of light

We'll sing all night

In a circle of light.

"Circle of Light" © Betsy Rose, available from Paper Crane Music, P.O. Box 9538, Berkely, CA 94709, 888-267-4833 (pin #8340).

Invitation to Session for Significant Others

Dear _____

In my work with survivors of childhood sexual abuse, I have learned how important relationships with significant others are in their healing process. To help you understand this process better, I invite you to an information session that through presentations, demonstrations, and handouts will answer the following questions:

- Why is a survivor of childhood sexual abuse diagnosed as having a posttraumatic stress disorder?

- Why does a survivor have repressed memories and what is now triggering recall?

- What is a shame-based family of origin and how does it affect an adult survivor?

- How does the process of dealing with the child within help healing?

- What can partners or significant others do to be supportive of the survivor's healing process?

Your confidentiality and that of our clients will be completely respected.

The fee for the session is _____ (insurance reimbursement is possible).

Please call _____ for more information or to register.

Sincerely,

©1998 Whole Person Associates 210 W Michigan Duluth MN 55802   (800) 247-6789

13 Session for Significant Others

Significant others may include partners, siblings, close friends, or relatives who have an interest in learning more about the effects of past abuse on the survivor and who would like to better understand the process of healing, particularly as it unfolds in the group process. Survivors use a letter to extend the invitation to whomever they wish to participate in this session. The survivors themselves do not attend the session. Facilitators must, therefore, respect their privacy and speak only in generic terms as they discuss particular themes in the healing process. Specific information about each survivor's story must be kept confidential.

Goals

To obtain information about childhood sexual abuse and its effects on adult survivors.

To learn how to provide support for survivors.

Materials

Easel pad and markers; **House Full of Secrets** handout; **Friends, Lovers, and Spouses of Survivors of Childhood Sexual Abuse** handout; **Characteristics of a Shame-Based Family handout**; audiotape player; audiotape with "House Full of Secrets"; audiotape with powerful orchestral music suitable as background for the earthquake visualization.

Introductions

As a nonthreatening warm-up activity that allows participants to share as little or as much as they want about themselves, ask them to talk for a minute about their first name, as was done in session 1 with survivors.

■ To help us become acquainted with each other, I'd like each of you to share your first name with the group along with a memory or association that is connected with your name.

■ You might want to tell us how you were given your name, who you were named after, or what you like or don't like about your name.

■ I'll begin by telling you about my first name.

After all participants have given their names, introduce the purpose of the session.

■ The purpose of this session is to give you, an important person in the life of a survivor of sexual abuse, the opportunity to learn more about the healing process.

■ Let's begin by listing the questions you would like to have answered by the end of this session.

> ☞*As participants call out their questions, write them on the easel paper.*

Understanding a house full of secrets

In order to help participants understand on a visceral level the pain survivors experience, distribute the **House Full of Secrets** handout (page 36) and ask them to follow along as you play the song.

Respond to participants' questions

Lead a discussion that weaves together the information you want to present and participants' questions, which are written on easel paper.

At appropriate times during the discussion distribute the **Friends, Lovers, and Spouses of Survivors of Childhood Sexual Abuse** and **Characteristics of a Shame-Based Family** handouts (page 39).

Be sure to respond in some way to all the questions that were listed and to additional ones that may surface.

Explaining the healing process

Help participants better understand the healing process by making some of the following points:

■ Although the abuse that happened to your loved one during her childhood was not your fault, you may still at times get the "residue" from that experience since you are living with a survivor of sexual abuse.

Explain that for survivors of sexual abuse to heal they must:

> ☞*Write these topics on easel paper as you state and comment on them.*

■ Remember the abuse

■ Tell about it (break the secret)

■ Feel the feelings that may have been repressed

■ Be validated by others both in the therapy group and in their own lives

■ Receive comfort and support from others and affirmation for having survived the abuse

> ☞*Sometimes, we also give to significant others the **DSM-IV Diagnosis for Post Traumatic Stress Disorder.***

Earthquake visualization

Address participants' feelings that they are unfairly affected by the abuse.

■ You may feel that your life is unfairly affected by events of the past, especially if you are involved in a sexual relationship with a survivor of abuse.

■ To help you better understand the effect this traumatic experience would have on a child, we'd like you to participate in a visualization. We used visualizations as a healing tool throughout the therapy sessions because they help people respond to feelings rather than just rational thoughts.

Begin with the relaxation script.

■ I'll begin with a script that will help you relax physically. After you have had time to relax, we will continue with a script that may help you feel some of the fear felt by a survivor of childhood sexual abuse. You will not be asked to visualize an abusive situation.

Give yourself permission to relax by sitting with your back supported and allow yourself to ground by putting both feet flat on the floor . . . As a way to turn inward, you may want to put your hands in your lap and let your chin rest on your chest . . .

When you feel your eyeids growing heavy, allow your eyes to close . . . a nice way to close out the outside world and feel even more grounded . . . focus inward and relax . . .

Give yourself permission to observe any sounds around you and know you can let them be . . .

Scan your body for tension. . . help it to be comfortable and relaxed . . .

Tune in now to your breathing . . . Notice your own rhythm and how its regularity can soothe you . . . Every once in a while you may wish to take a deep cleansing breath . . . inhaling through your nose and exhaling slowly through your mouth . . . Notice the moment of inner peace at the top of the in-breath before you exhale . . .

This time . . . as you exhale . . . blow out as though you're making a candle flame flicker with your breath . . . long, slow exhale without blowing out the flame . . . again . . . and again.

Continue to breathe slowly as I set the mood with music and begin the visualization.

Take youself back in time, farther and farther back until you are, in your imagination, five years old . . . Remember what it was like to be that small . . . that dependent on adults for everything you need . . .

Now imagine yourself, still as a five-year-old child in the city of San Francisco . . . You find yourself separated from your family, alone on a cable car at the top of one of the city's steepest hills. You look down and see the city at your feet.

Suddenly, the cable car begins to shake, at first just a little bit, then more and more violently. Around you, houses are collapsing. Close by, fires are consuming homes and shops. You see the destruction all around, but you don't understand what is happening. You're all alone, and you feel terrified and helpless . . . Allow yourself to feel the child's terror . . allow it to build as you stand trembling on the cable car, all alone . . . (pause, then allow the music to fade slowly).

When you are ready, stretch and open your eyes but remain silent as you think about what it would have been like if you had experienced such an earthquake when you were five years old.

Imagine now that you are an adult, living on the East Coast, far away from San Francisco, having almost forgotten that terribly frightening experience from your childhood. Suddenly, the earth trembles . . . just a little . . and the fear washes over you again. Logically, you know it's not a real earthquake, but the feelings of terror and helplessness are just as real as they were many years ago.

For a few moments longer, reflect on the fear and betrayal and loneliness felt by a child who is being sexually abused . . . Just as a few tremors can bring back to an adult the fear connected with an earthquake, intimacy can cause an adult who was sexually abused to recall and refeel their childhood experience.

Conclude the educational part of this session by asking for discussion of the visualization. Encourage participants to remember this experience and to be patient and supportive if their loved one fears intimacy, recognizing that these fears may actually increase temporarily during the healing process.

Closing ritual

Invite participants to stand in a circle as the survivors did at the close of each session. If concerns surface, be ready to make suggestions and offer resources.

■ Before our session ends, please share with the group any thoughts or concerns that you may have as a result of this experience.

■ Let's stand silently for moment as we honor the courage of your loved ones, knowing that for them to heal often means making a commitment to once again experience the terror of intimacy.

Friends, Lovers, and Spouses of Survivors of Childhood Sexual Abuse

You are IMPORTANT to a survivor's healing . . .

Remember to . . .

Believe her
Her greatest fear is that you won't.

Stay on her side
She needs to hear from you that it was not her fault.

Listen to her
She has remained quiet for too long.

Accept her feelings
They have been negated, distorted, and invalidated too often.

Support and encourage her
This will help her heal.

Challenge her on self-sabotaging behavior
She may need your protection and your loving feedback.

Educate yourself about the effects of child abuse.

Honor the time, energy, and resources she invests in her healing.
This will benefit you as well as her.

©1998 Whole Person Associates 210 W Michigan Duluth MN 55802   (800) 247-6789

P.T.S.D.—Posttraumatic Stress Disorder

Adult survivors of childhood incest are often diagnosed with post-traumatic stress disorder.

This diagnosis results from the survivor's exposure to a traumatic event (sexual abuse) and its result: intense fear, helplessness, or horror. This diagnosis is also commonly used for soldiers who were traumatized by war. The following are common characteristics experienced by those diagnosed with posttraumatic stress disorder:

The reexperiencing of the traumatic event (in this case, sexual abuse) often occurs in one or more of the following ways:

1. Recurrent memories or thoughts

2. Recurring dreams

3. Recurring flashbacks

4. Intense physical and/or psychological feelings when experiencing memories, dreams, or flashbacks.

Survivors often avoid the intense feelings associated with this trauma by:

1. Avoiding thoughts, feelings, or conversations about the trauma

2. Avoiding activities, places, and people associated with the trauma

3. Forgetting the abuse

4. Detaching from others

5. Not planning for the future

Common symptoms include sleep problems, irritability, anger outbursts, difficulty concentrating, and hyper-vigilance.

Resources

References

Introduction

Briere, J., & Runtz, M. (1988). Symptomology Associated With Childhood Sexual Victimization in a Non-clinical Adult Sample. *Child Abuse and Neglect*, 12, pp. 51–59.

Finkelhor, D., (1990). Early and Long-term Effects of Child Sexual Abuse: An Update, *Professional Psychology: Research and Practice*, 21, pp. 325–330.

Freeman-Longo & Blanchard, G., (1997). *Sexual Abuse in America: Epidemic of the 21st Century*, Safer Society Press, Brandon, Vt.

Session 1

Dolan, Y. (1991). The Legacy of Abuse. *Resolving Sexual Abuse*, N.Y.: Norton, Chapter 1.

Frances, A. & First, M, EDS. (1994). Posttraumatic Stress Disorder. *Diagnostic Criteria from DSMIV*, Washington, D.C.: American Psychiatric Association, pp. 209–221.

Vanderbuilt, H. (1992). Incest—A Chilling Report. *Lear's*, pp. 18–49.

Williams, M. (1993). Establishing Safety in Survivor's of Severe Sexual Abuse in PTS Therapy Part II and Part III. *Treating Abuse Today*, 3.

Session 2

Courtois, C. (1992). The Memory Retrieval Process in Incest Survivor Therapy. *Journal of Child Sexual Abuse*, 1, pp. 15–31.

Dolan, Y. (1991). Seeding Hope: Utilizing the Client's Resources. *Resolving Sexual Abuse,* N.Y.: Norton, Chapter II.

Session 5

Karen, Robert (1992, February). Shame. *The Atlantic Monthly,* pp. 40–70.

Session 6

Bradshaw, J. (1990). Liberating Your Lost Inner Child. *Reclaiming the Inner Child,* N.Y.: Tarcher, pp. 224–233.

Session 7

Capacchione (1990). The Power of Your Other Hand. *Reclaiming the Inner Child,* Calif.: Tarcher, pp. 209–216.

Cohen, B. (1992). Art in Therapy by Non-Specialists. *Treating Your Abuse Today,* 2, (No. 4), pp. 13–14.

Session 8

Lerner, H. (1985). The Challenge of Anger. *The Dance of Anger,* N.Y.: Perennial Library, pp. 1–16.

Tarvis, C. (1982). Getting It Out of Your System—Myths of Expressed Anger. *Anger,* N.Y.: Touchstone Book, pp. 120–150.

Session 9

Forward, S. (1989). Confrontation: The Road to Independence. *Toxic Parents,* N.Y.: Bantam Books, pp. 236–274.

Session 11

Bass, E. & Davis, L. (1988). Grieving and Mourning. *The Courage to Heal,* N.Y.: Harper and Row, pp. 118–121

Samford, Lynn (1990). *Strong at Broken Places: Overcoming the Trauma of Childhood Abuse*, N.Y.: Avon Books.

Wolter, D. (1989). *Forgiving Our Parents: For Adult Children of Dysfunctional Families,* Minn.: CompCare Publishers, pp. 21–28.

Session 13

Graber, K. (1991). *Ghosts in the Bedroom: A Guide for Partners of Incest Survivors*, Fla.: Health Communications, pp. 95–124.

Introduction to Using Guided Imagery

If you are not familiar with using guided meditations, this brief introduction will provide the information you need to begin.

Everyone is different, so each participant will experience guided imagery uniquely. These individual differences should be encouraged. During a guided meditation, some people will imagine vivid scenes, colors, images, or sounds while others will focus on what they are feeling. This is why a combination of sights, sounds, and feelings have been incorporated into the scripts. With practice, it is possible to expand your participants' range of awareness.

By careful selection of images you can help deepen their experience and cultivate their awareness in new areas that can enrich their lives. For instance, people who are most comfortable in the visual area can be encouraged to stretch their awareness and increase their sensitivity to feelings and sounds.

Prepare the individual by physically relaxing her, which reduces anxiety, activates the creative right brain, and enhances the ability to concentrate on mental images. Some type of physical relaxation sequence should be used prior to any guided meditation.

Breathing properly is essential for complete and total relaxation. Unfortunately, very few people take full breaths, especially when under stress. When a person consciously takes deep breaths, stress is reduced and the mind can remain calm and in control. It is important that people focus on their breathing, taking in full deep breaths through their nose and exhaling through their mouth.

Before beginning any guided meditation, briefly describe the images you will use and ask if they make anyone feel uncomfortable. People who are afraid of water may find images of ocean waves to be frightening rather than calming. Be prepared to go with an alternate image. Let participants know that if they become uncomfortable, they may, at any time, open their eyes and tune out the visualization.

Choose the right atmosphere. Select a room that has comfortable chairs for sitting or a carpeted floor for lying down. Close the door and shut the windows to block out distracting noises. Custom select music to support your goals whenever possible. You may want to follow the tips on page 99.

If possible, dim the lights to create a relaxing environment. Low lights enhance the ability to relax by blocking out visual distraction. If distractions occur—a noisy air conditioner, traffic, loud conversations—try raising your voice, using shorter phrases and fewer pauses, or incorporating the sounds into the guided meditation. For example, you might say, "Notice how the humming sounds of the air conditioner relax you more and more," or "If your mind begins to drift, gently bring it back to the sound of my voice."

Speak in a calm, comforting, and steady manner. Let your voice flow. Your voice should be smooth and somewhat monotonous—but don't whisper. Pace yourself so that you read the guided meditations slowly, but not so slowly that you lose people. Begin at a conversational pace and slow down as the relaxation progresses. It's easy to go too fast, so take your time. Don't rush.

Give participants time to follow your instructions. If you suggest that they wiggle their toes, watch them do so, then wait for them to stop wiggling their toes before going on. When your participants are relaxed and engaged in the imagery process, they have tapped into their subconscious mind (slow, rich, imagery)—and they shouldn't be hurried.

As you reach the end of a meditation, help participants make the transition back to the present. Tell them to visualize their surroundings, to stretch, and to breathe deeply. Repeat these instructions until everyone is alert.

Adapted from *30 Scripts for Relaxation, Imagery, & Inner Healing*, Vol. 1, © 1992 Julie Lusk, Whole Person Associates.

Tips on Music Selection

- Choose music that has flowing melodies rather than disjointed and fragmented melodies.

- Don't assume that the type of music you find relaxing will be relaxing to others. Have a variety of musical styles available and ask your clients for suggestions.

- Try using sounds from nature like ocean waves. Experiment with New Age music and Space music, much of which is appropriate for relaxation work. Classical music may be effective, especially movements that are marked 'largo' or 'adagio.'

- Adjust the volume so that it doesn't drown out your voice. On the other hand, music that is too soft may cause your listeners to strain to hear it.

- Select music based upon the mood desired. Sedative music is soothing and produces a contemplative mood. Stimulative music increases bodily energy and stimulates the emotions.

- Select music with a slow tempo and low pitch. The higher the pitch or frequency of sound the more likely it will be irritating.

Imagery Vividness Scale

The Imagery Vividness Scale is a useful, nonthreatening way to make clients aware of their own potential for visualization. You may want to use it before starting any imagery work. Be aware that visualization is a positive reframing of dissociation at which most survivors of trauma are very skilled.

If you decide to use the scale in the group setting, either photocopy and distribute the worksheet on the following page, or write the scale on easel paper and distribute blank paper and pencils. Then read each statement, giving enough time for participants to imagine the scene before moving to the next one. Conclude the exercise by asking which scenes were easiest and most difficult to visualize.

Alternatively, participants could be asked to complete the worksheet as part of a homework assignment.

Imagine This . . .

4—Very clear, 3—Moderately clear, 2—Fairly clear, 1—Unclear

1. See a friend standing in front of you.   _____

2. Imagine her or him laughing.   _____

3. Picture his or her eyes.   _____

4. Visualize a bowl of fruit.   _____

5. Imagine driving down a dry, dusty road.   _____

6. See yourself throwing a ball.   _____

7. See a white, sandy beach.

8. Picture your childhood home.   _____

9. Imagine looking into a shop window.   _____

10. See a blank television screen.   _____

11. Imagine the sound of an exploding firecracker.   _____

12. Imagine the sound of a barking dog.   _____

13. Feel the warmth of a hot shower.   _____

14. Imagine feeling the texture of rough sandpaper.   _____

15. Picture yourself lifting a heavy object.   _____

16. Imagine yourself walking up a steep stairway.   _____

17. Imagine the taste of lemon juice.   _____

18. Think of eating ice cream.   _____

19. Imagine the smell of cooking cabbage.   _____

20. Imagine yourself smelling a rose.   _____

TOTAL   _____

Adapted from *In the Mind's Eye*, © 1977 Arnold Lazarus, PhD.

Managed Care Organizations

Managed care organizations typically require clinical assessments and short-term, solution-focused treatments plans.

We have developed a record keeping system that organizes relevant information for treatment purposes and also provides the information required by managed care organizations. We share them with you for your adaptation.

Included in this section are samples and instructions for the following forms:

1. Telephone intake

2. Initial individual assessment process

3. Treatment plan design (both group and individual)

4. Telephonic managed care organization review

5. Follow-up letter to demonstrate treatment results

Telephone Intake

It is very important that the intake worker be sensitive to how difficult it is for a survivor to make a phone call to be part of a group for survivors of sexual abuse. The form we use is attached, but we ask our intake worker to remain flexible and supportive to the caller. If the client finds it difficult to talk, we ask the worker to take down the basic information first. Going over the phone number, address, etc. allows time for the caller to relax with familiar information and gives the intake worker time to establish rapport and put the caller at ease. If the client is still unable to talk about why she is calling, our intake worker (who is not a therapist) arranges for a therapist to call her back and do further assessment.

It has been our experience that if one of our colleagues has referred this client to us, she's probably ready for this group.

An intake worker must respect confidentiality while getting a very brief statement of how the client sees her problem. Her description often assists us in assessing whether the client is appropriate for our group. It is important that while being sensitive and understanding, the intake worker does not allow the client to get into details of the abuse. A brief statement of the fact that abuse occurred and that she has worked on it in individual counseling is enough at this time.

To help us to assess a caller's readiness for our group, we like our intake worker to write down her impressions and comments after the call.

Telephone Intake for
Survivors of Childhood Sexual Abuse Group

Date intake done: _____

Intake worker: _____

Name_____

Address _____

City/State/Zip _____

Referred by: _____

Client home phone: _____

Client work phone: _____

Best time to call: _____

Information concerning confidentiality:_____

_____

_____

_____

Relationship status:

❏ Married   Spouse's Name: _____

❏ Divorced   ❏ Single   ❏ Living together

Partner's name: _____

Children (names and ages): _____

_____

Family of origin history (identify perpetrator of abuse and age at onset as well as duration of abuse) _____

_____

_____

Personal information:

Client's DOB: _____

Who lives with client: _____

_____

Currently employed: ❏ No   ❏ Yes

Where _____

Position _____

Health insurance information: _____

_____

Insurance number: _____

Previous counseling: _____

When? who? how long? for what issues? _____

_____

_____

_____

Current as well as past history of medications: (esp. medications prescribed for anxiety, depression, and insomnia) _____

_____

_____

_____

Brief statement of problem (in client's words if possible): _____

_____

_____

_____

_____

_____

Comments of intake worker: _____

_____

_____

_____

_____

_____

Next step: _____

_____

_____

_____

_____

Initial Assessment

We always arrange for both facilitators to be present during an individual assessment for each client who applies to be in our group. We spend at least 1/2 hour with each survivor. During this time, we assess her readiness for a group experience and give her the opportunity to get to know us.

The following questions need to be answered during this initial interview:

1. Can this person tell her story of abuse to us? If she cannot, she may not be ready for the group and we encourage her to continue in individual therapy.

2. What are her goals for the group?

3. What does she see as her strengths and challenges in participating in a group?

4. Does she have any questions of us? We respond to any questions that are asked. We are open about our credentials, and we explain that neither of us experienced abuse as children. We do not believe that a history of child abuse is a requirement for facilitators; neither do we believe that it is an impediment. We share this information with survivors because we believe that our being authentic encourages trust.

5. What is the nature of the survivor's family of origin? We also obtain a brief overview of family-of-origin history by using a lifeline and genogram. See page 108.

We obtain a release of confidentiality so that we may talk to the client's individual therapist if necessary. However, we explain to each client that, even with this written release, we never at anytime during the group, speak to an individual therapist without first discussing it with our client. These survivors come from families where secrets were common and we do not want to perpetuate such behavior.

Genogram

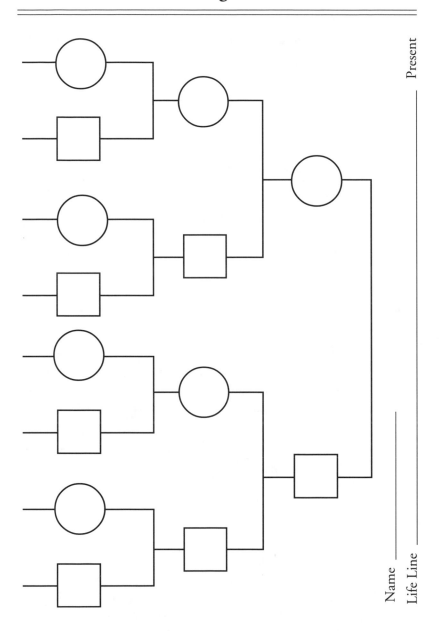

The genogram is a useful tool for gathering family data in the initial interview. See McGoldrick, M., (1985) *Genograms in Family Assessment,* N.Y.: WW Norton & Gerson, Randy.

How to use the Genogram

During the assessment session, the following information should be obtained and recorded on the Genogram.

- Names and ages of as many family members as possible.

- Family history of alcoholism, treated or not.

- Family history of mental illness, treated or not.

- Alliances and cutoffs between family members.

- Important events both positive and negative (record this information on the lifeline).

- Any physical, sexual, or emotional abuse among family members in addition to the abuse experienced by the survivor.

©1998 Whole Person Associates 210 W Michigan Duluth MN 55802   (800) 247-6789

Authorization for
Release of Confidential Information

I hereby authorize (group facilitator's name) to consult with:

Name of therapist: _____

Address: _____

City/State/Zip: _____

Phone: _____

Purpose or need for information: Counseling in a 12-session group for survivors of childhood sexual abuse.

~ ~ ~ ~

I understand this consent may be withdrawn by me at any time except to the extent that action has been taken and that it will automatically be withdrawn at the end of this 12-session group.

_____

Signature of client   Date

_____

Witness (usually the therapist)   Date

©1998 Whole Person Associates 210 W Michigan Duluth MN 55802   (800) 247-6789

Treatment Plan Recording

After each group session, both therapists discuss and process their impressions and then document them. We also make a note for each individual client, recording the progress she has made toward her goals.

Halfway through the group sessions and at the last session we often ask clients to consider the progress they have made toward each goal. They rank their progress on a scale from 1 to 10. These numbers are written on the list of goals that are posted on the wall at each group meeting.

In addition to the above, after each session we also make a group note of homework assigned and the plan for the next session.

We believe it is important to write the notes immediately following each group session. This encourages the documentation of general impressions as well as development of goals for the next session. This debriefing also allows facilitators to let go of group material, issues, and emotional responses, which can help to minimize the vicarious traumatization often experienced by professionals working with this population.

Telephone MCO Review

Following is a form that we complete before talking with managed care organizations. It is important to note that we always use the DSMIV of 309.81 PTSD diagnosis on Axis I for survivors of sexual abuse. We also confer with the survivor's individual therapist for a more complete diagnosis on Axes II–IV unless there are significant, notable characteristics that become apparent at our initial assessment.

The number of sessions we are requesting and the treatment goals are always the same as noted on our form.

It may be important to note that many insurance companies will only pay for therapy that is medically necessary and therefore any symptoms that interfere with daily or job-related functioning (such as trouble concentrating, sleep disfunction, etc.) should be noted.

MCO Telephone Review

Patient's name: _____

Insured ID#: _____

Insured DOB: _____

Patient's date of birth: _____

Patient's SS#: _____

DSMIV: _____

_____

_____

Diagnosis	Axis I <u>309.81, PTSD</u>	pp. 209–211
Personality Disorder	Axis II _____	p. 275
Medical Condition	Axis III _____	p. 39
Source of Problems	Axis IV _____	pp. 42–43
Functioning	Axis V _____	(GAF) pp. 46–48

* Page numbers refer to descriptions in APA's 1994 *Quick Reference to the Diagnostic Criteria From DSMIV*, Washington, D.C.

Number of sessions requested: <u>12 group sessions</u>

<u>(1–1/2 hours each); maximum of 7 participants per group</u>

Brief overview of symptoms: _____

_____

_____

Presenting problem: _____

_____

_____

_____

Functional impairments: _____

_____

_____

_____

Treatment goals: <u>Identify as a survivor (as opposed to a victim) and recover from childhood trauma.</u>

Notes

Talked to: _____

Date: _____

Number of sessions approved: _____

Dates of sessions: _____

Demonstrating Treatment Results

To help support the clinical effectiveness of our treatment, we evaluate the group in several ways.

First, we schedule session 12, our last session, from two weeks to a month after session 11. This allows clients time for integrating what they have absorbed from the group. At the 12th session, they are asked to comment on that integration.

Also, we offer a 13th session for significant others in our clients' lives (as noted in main text.) These people often give us feedback as to the group's effectiveness for their partners and their relationship with them.

Finally, we mail a survey about three months after the group terminates. This helps us plan for future groups. You will find a sample letter on the following page.

We often get unsolicited cards and letters from our group members, which we save as further evidence of the group's effectiveness.

Follow-Up Letter

Date:

Dear _____,

We hope this letter finds you healthy and happy. We are writing to ask you for feedback on your group experience with us.

Would you just answer two questions for us?

1. What helped you most in your survivor group?

2. What are the challenges you face today in your healing process?

Enclosed is a self-addressed, stamped envelope for your convenience. You may send this to us anonymously or signed. As always, we will respect your confidentiality and we value your input.

Thank you so much,

Bonnie Collins and Kathy Marsh

WHOLE PERSON ASSOCIATES RESOURCES

Our materials are designed to address the whole person—physical, emotional, mental, spiritual, and social. Developed for trainers by trainers, all of these resources are ready-to-use. Novice trainers will find everything they need to get started, and the expert trainer will discover new ideas and concepts to add to their existing programs.

GROUP PROCESS RESOURCES

All of the exercises in our group process resources encourage interaction between the leader and participants, as well as among the participants. Each exercise includes everything you need to present a meaningful program: goals, optimal group size, time frame, materials list, and the complete process instructions.

WORKING WITH GROUPS FROM DYSFUNCTIONAL FAMILIES

Cheryl Hetherington

This collection of 29 proven group activities is designed to heal the pain that results from growing up in or living in a dysfunctional family. With these exercises you can:

- promote healing
- build self-esteem
- encourage sharing
- help participants acknowledge their feelings

WORKING WITH GROUPS FROM DYSFUNCTIONAL FAMILIES REPRODUCIBLE WORKSHEET MASTERS

A complete package of full-size (8 1/2" x 11") photocopy masters that include all the worksheets and handouts from **Working with Groups from Dysfunctional Families** is available to you. Use the masters for easy duplication of the handouts for each participant.

❏ **DFHN / Working with Groups from Dysfunctional Families / $24.95**
❏ **DFW / Dysfunctional Families Worksheet Masters / $9.95**

©1998 Whole Person Associates 210 W Michigan Duluth MN 55802   (800) 247-6789

MORE GROUP PROCESS RESOURCES

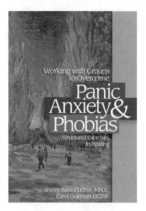

WORKING WITH GROUPS TO OVERCOME PANIC, ANXIETY, & PHOBIAS

Shirley Babior, LCSW, MFCC, and
Carol Goldman, LICSW

Written especially for therapists and group leaders, this manual presents well-researched, state-of-the-art treatment strategies and action-oriented client activities for a variety of anxiety disorders including:

● panic disorder
● generalized anxiety
● agoraphobia, social anxiety
● specific phobias, such as fear of flying

Sample treatment plans with behavioral goals and objectives make this book a priceless resource for therapists who must develop and document appropriate treatment protocols and strategies for clients served by managed-care organizations. Adapt your presentation for individual or group therapy or for worksite lectures and all-day workshops—the book's format makes it easy. Support groups also will find this manual helpful.

❑ GPP / Working with Groups to Overcome Panic, Anxiety, & Phobias / $24.95
❑ GPPW / Worksheet Masters / $9.95

About the authors
Shirley Babior, a psychotherapist in private practice in San Diego, California, is codirector of the Center for Anxiety and Stress Treatment. Carol Goldman, a founding director of the Boston Institute of Cognitive-Behavior Therapies, is a therapist in private practice in Boston, Massachusetts.

OVERCOMING PANIC, ANXIETY, & PHOBIAS
Strategies to Free Yourself from Worry and Fear

Shirley Babior, LCSW, MFCC, and
Carol Goldman, LICSW

This practical handbook, recommended by experts in the field of anxiety disorders for people whose lives are upset by worry, fear, or panic, offers coping strategies based on the latest clinical research. Personal stories of recovery, worksheets for recording symptoms and progress, and information on finding professional help make this book a must-read for anxiety sufferers who want to regain control of their life.

❑ OPAP / Overcoming Panic, Anxiety, &
   Phobias / $12.95

A 10-WEEK RECOVERY PROGRAM FOR OVERCOMING PANIC, ANXIETY, & PHOBIAS

Shirley Babior, LCSW, MFCC, and
Carol Goldman, LICSW

State-of-the-art cognitive-behavioral strategies endorsed by leading clinical experts provide panic relief and help listeners learn the skills they need to manage anxiety disorders before the problem gets out of control. This six-tape program also is ideal for helping clients reduce chronic stress and tension. The program includes:

- six audiotapes (ten instructional sessions plus the *Calm Down* tape, which features four relaxation scripts)
- worksheets with homework assignments to support each session
- *Overcoming Panic, Anxiety, & Phobias*, a practical self-help handbook of coping strategies

❏ **PRP / 10-Week Recovery Program (six audiotapes, book, worksheets) / $95.00**

Therapists: Call for quantity discounts on 10-Week Recovery Programs for your clients.

WORRY STOPPERS

Breathing & Imagery to
Calm the Restless Mind
audiotape

These six calming visualization exercises will help you learn new ways to breathe, relax, clear your mind, and release tension.

❏ **WS / Worry Stoppers / $11.95**

CALM DOWN

Relaxation & Imagery Skills for
Managing Fear, Anxiety, Panic
audiotape

Turn off the panic button, breathe away stress, and experience total body relaxation.

❏ **CALM / Calm Down / $11.95**

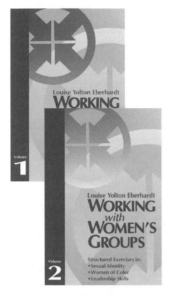

WORKING WITH WOMEN'S GROUPS VOLUMES 1 & 2
Louise Yolton Eberhardt

The two volumes of **Working with Women's Groups** have been completely revised and updated. These exercises will help women explore issues that are of perennial concern as well as today's hot topics.

Volume 1:
- consciousness-raising
- self-discovery
- assertiveness training

Volume 2:
- sexuality issues
- women of color
- leadership skills training

WORKING WITH WOMEN'S GROUPS WORKSHEET MASTERS

Complete packages of full-size (8 1/2" x 11") photocopy masters that include all the worksheets and handouts from **Working with Women's Groups volumes 1 and 2** are available to you. Use the masters for easy duplication of the handouts for each participant.

❏ **WG1N / Working with Women's Groups, Vol. 1 / $24.95**
❏ **WG2N / Working with Women's Groups, Vol. 2 / $24.95**
❏ **WG1W / Working with Women's Groups, Vol. 1 Worksheet Masters / $9.95**
❏ **WG2W / Working with Women's Groups, Vol. 2 Worksheet Masters / $9.95**

WORKING WITH MEN'S GROUPS
Roger Karsk and Bill Thomas

Also revised and updated, this volume is a valuable resource for anyone working with men's groups. The exercises cover a variety of topics, including:

- self discovery
- parenting
- conflict
- intimacy

❏ **MGN / Working with Men's Groups / $24.95**
❏ **MGW / Working with Men's Groups Worksheet Masters / $9.95**

WELLNESS ACTIVITIES FOR YOUTH VOLUMES 1 & 2

Sandy Queen

Each volume of **Wellness Activities for Youth** helps leaders teach children and teenagers about wellness with a whole person approach, a "no put-down" rule, and most of all, an emphasis on FUN. The concepts include:

- values
- stress and coping
- self-esteem
- personal well-being
- social wellness

WELLNESS ACTIVITIES FOR YOUTH WORKSHEET MASTERS

Complete packages of full-size (8 1/2" x 11") photocopy masters that include all the worksheets and handouts from **Wellness Activities for Youth Volumes 1 and 2** are available to you. Use the masters for easy duplication of the handouts for each participant.

❏ WY1 / Wellness Activities for Youth, Vol. 1 / $21.95
❏ WY2 / Wellness Activities for Youth, Vol. 2 / $21.95
❏ WY1W / Wellness Activities for Youth, Vol. 1 Worksheet Masters / $9.95
❏ WY2W / Wellness Activities for Youth, Vol. 2 Worksheet Masters / $9.95

PLAYFUL ACTIVITIES FOR POWERFUL PRESENTATIONS

Bruce Williamson

This book contains 40 fun exercises designed to fit any group or topic. These exercises will help you:

- build teamwork
- encourage laughter and playfulness
- relieve stress and tension
- free up the imaginations of participants

❏ **PAP / Playful Activities for Powerful Presentations / $21.95**

WORKSHOPS-IN-A-BOOK

KICKING YOUR STRESS HABITS:
A DO-IT-YOURSELF GUIDE TO COPING WITH STRESS
Donald A. Tubesing, PhD

Over a quarter of a million people have found ways to deal with their everyday stress by using **Kicking Your Stress Habits**. This workshop-in-a-book actively involves the reader in assessing stressful patterns and developing more effective coping strategies with helpful "Stop and Reflect" sections in each chapter.

The 10-step planning process and 20 skills for managing stress make **Kicking Your Stress Habits** an ideal text for stress management classes in many different settings, from hospitals to universities and for a wide variety of groups.

❑ **K / Kicking Your Stress Habits / $15.95**

SEEKING YOUR HEALTHY BALANCE:
A DO-IT-YOURSELF GUIDE TO WHOLE PERSON WELL-BEING
Donald A. Tubesing, PhD, and Nancy Loving Tubesing, EdD

Where can you find the time and energy to "do it all" without sacrificing your health and well-being? **Seeking Your Healthy Balance** helps the reader discover how to make changes toward a more balanced lifestyle by learning effective ways to juggle work, self, and others; clarifying self-care options; and discovering and setting their own personal priorities.

Seeking Your Healthy Balance asks the questions and helps readers find their own answers.

❑ **HB / Seeking Your Healthy Balance / $15.95**

©1998 Whole Person Associates 210 W Michigan Duluth MN 55802   (800) 247-6789

RELAXATION RESOURCES

Many trainers and workshop leaders have discovered the benefits of relaxation and visualization in healing the body, mind, and spirit.

30 SCRIPTS FOR RELAXATION, IMAGERY, AND INNER HEALING
Julie Lusk

These two volumes are collections of relaxation scripts created by trainers for trainers. The 30 scripts in each of the two volumes have been professionally-tested and fine-tuned so they are ready to use for both novice and expert trainers.

Help your participants change their behavior, enhance their self-esteem, discover inner, private places, and heal themselves through simple trainer-led guided imagery scripts. Both volumes include information on how to use the scripts, suggestions for tailoring them to your specific needs and audience, and information on how to successfully incorporate guided imagery into your existing programs.

❏ 30S / 30 Scripts for Relaxation, Imagery, and Inner Healing, Vol. 1 / $21.95
❏ 30S2 / 30 Scripts for Relaxation, Imagery, and Inner Healing, Vol. 2 / $21.95

INQUIRE WITHIN
Andrew Schwartz

Use visualization to make positive changes in your life. The 24 visualization experiences in **Inquire Within** will help participants enhance their creativity, heal inner pain, learn to relax, and deal with conflict. Each visualization includes questions at the end of the process that encourage deeper reflection and a better understanding of the exercise and the response it invokes.

❏ IW / Inquire Within / $21.95

©1998 Whole Person Associates 210 W Michigan Duluth MN 55802   (800) 247-6789

RELAXATION AUDIOTAPES—$11.95 EACH

Perhaps you're an old hand at relaxation, looking for new ideas. Or maybe you're a beginner, just testing the waters. Whatever your relaxation needs, Whole Person tapes provide a whole family of techniques for reducing physical and mental stress. All are carefully crafted to promote whole person relaxation—body, mind, and spirit. We also provide a line of music-only tapes, composed specifically for relaxation.

SENSATIONAL RELAXATION

When stress piles up, it becomes a heavy load both physically and emotionally. Experience the liberating power of stress relief with these full-length relaxation experiences. Each appeals to the senses and teaches specific relaxation techniques and skills that can be used again and again.

❑ **CD / Countdown to Relaxation**   ❑ **RLX / Relax . . . Let Go . . . Relax**
❑ **DS / Daybreak / Sundown**   ❑ **SRL / StressRelease**
❑ **TDB / Take a Deep Breath**   ❑ **WRM / Warm and Heavy**

STRESS BREAKS

Do you need a short energy booster or a quick stress reliever? If you don't know what type of relaxation you like, or if you are new to guided relaxation techniques, try one of our Stress Breaks for a quick refocusing or change of pace any time of the day.

❑ **BT / BreakTime**   ❑ **WS / Worry Stoppers**
❑ **NT / Natural Tranquilizers**   ❑ **CALM / Calm Down**
❑ **SE / Stress Escapes**

MINI-MEDITATION

These brief guided visualizations begin with focusing your breathing and uncluttering your mind so that you can concentrate on a sequence of sensory images that promote relaxation, centering, healing, and growth.

❑ **RJ / Refreshing Journeys**
❑ **HV / Healing Visions**
❑ **HC / Healthy Choices**

WILDERNESS DAYDREAMS

Discover the healing power of nature with the four tapes in the Wilderness Daydreams series. The eight special journeys will transport you from your harried, stressful surroundings to the peaceful serenity of words and water.

❑ **WD1 / Canoe / Rain**
❑ **WD2 / Island /Spring**
❑ **WD3 / Campfire / Stream**
❑ **WD4 / Sailboat / Pond**

©1998 Whole Person Associates 210 W Michigan Duluth MN 55802   (800) 247-6789

DAYDREAMS
Escape from the stress around you with guided tours to beautiful places. Picture yourself traveling to the ocean, sitting in a park, luxuriating in the view from the majestic mountains, or enjoying the solitude and serenity of a cozy cabin. The 10-minute escapes included in our Daydream tapes will lead your imagination away from your everyday cares so you can resume your tasks relaxed and comforted.

- ❑ DD1 / Daydreams 1: Getaways
- ❑ DD2 / Daydreams 2: Peaceful Places
- ❑ DD3 / Daydreams 3: Relaxing Retreats

GUIDED MEDITATION
Take a step beyond relaxation and discover the connection between body and mind with guided meditation. The imagery in our full-length meditations will help you discover your strengths, find healing, make positive life changes, and recognize your inner wisdom.

- ❑ IH / Inner Healing
- ❑ PE / Personal Empowering
- ❑ HBT / Healthy Balancing
- ❑ SPC / Spiritual Centering
- ❑ MT / Mantras

DO-IT-YOURSELF WELLNESS
Tap in to your natural wellness resources with guided imagery and movement that enhance whole person well-being: body, mind, and spirit. These unusual tapes include daily self-care routines that promote a healthy lifestyle as they melt away tension and affirm your own inner wisdom.

- ❑ BI / Body Image
- ❑ E / Eating
- ❑ MA / Massage
- ❑ Y / Yoga

MUSIC ONLY
No relaxation program would be complete without relaxing melodies that can be played as background to a prepared script or that can be enjoyed as you practice a technique you have already learned. Steven Eckels composed his melodies specifically for relaxation. These "musical prayers for healing" will calm your body, mind, and spirit.

- ❑ T / Tranquility
- ❑ H / Harmony
- ❑ S / Serenity
- ❑ CTCD / Contemplation CD / $15.95

Titles can be combined for discounts!